Routledge Revivals

Teaching History from Primary Evidence

Originally published in 1993, this volume will be of particular interest to primary school teachers who may never have taught history as a discreet subject before and who are worried by their negative memories of school history and lack confidence as to their own knowledge of the subject. The author provides a practical guide to the theory and rudiments of history with guidance on how to present it using primary evidence in an exciting way that makes sense in terms of primary practice.

Teaching History from Primary Evidence

Keith Andreetti

First published in 1993
by David Fulton Publishers Ltd

This edition first published in 2018 by Routledge
2 Park Square, Milton Park, Abingdon, Oxon, OX14 4RN
and by Routledge
605 Third Avenue, New York, NY 10017

Routledge is an imprint of the Taylor & Francis Group, an informa business

© 1993 Keith Andreetti

All rights reserved. No part of this book may be reprinted or reproduced or utilised in any form or by any electronic, mechanical, or other means, now known or hereafter invented, including photocopying and recording, or in any information storage or retrieval system, without permission in writing from the publishers.

Publisher's Note
The publisher has gone to great lengths to ensure the quality of this reprint but points out that some imperfections in the original copies may be apparent.

Disclaimer
The publisher has made every effort to trace copyright holders and welcomes correspondence from those they have been unable to contact.

A Library of Congress record exists under LCCN: 93224898

ISBN 13: 978-1-138-50563-6 (hbk)
ISBN 13: 978-1-315-14668-3 (ebk)
ISBN 13: 978-1-138-50570-4 (pbk)

DOI: 10.4324/9781315146683

David Fulton Publishers Ltd
2 Barbon Close, London WC1N 3JX

First published in Great Britain by
David Fulton Publishers 1993

Note: The right of the author to be identified as the author of this work has been asserted by him in accordance with the Copyright, Designs and Patents Act 1988.

Copyright © Keith Andreetti

British Library Cataloguing in Publication Data

A catalogue record for this book is available from the British Library

ISBN 1-85346-183-0

All rights reserved. No part of this publication may be reproduced, stored in a retrieval system or transmitted, in any form, or by any means, electronic, mechanical, photocopying, recording or otherwise, without the prior permission of the publishers.

Typeset by Witwell Ltd, Southport

Contents

1 What is History?..1
2 How to Look at Artefacts..10
3 Artefacts in Context..23
4 Using Museums...33
5 Experimental Archaeology..45
6 Oral History..57
7 Documentary Evidence...67
8 Planning a History Study Unit..79
   Index..89

CHAPTER 1
What is History?

> I know something about history. I know when I am being threatened.
> Edward Albee.

It may be asked why so many books on the subject of history find it necessary to commence by defining their discipline, at least at such length as many such books do. The answer is, I think, that history is a very powerful force that works on the consciousness of every human being on the planet, and it is at its most powerful when we do not think too hard about its nature: we are conditioned, therefore, not to do so.

As I write news broadcasts are once again focused on 'the Palestinian Problem'. Israeli leaders affirm the historical rights of the Jewish people to the land of Israel. Their arguments are based on the pre-Roman location of Hebrew- and Aramaic-speaking states in that area, and more cogently to its centrality in their religion. They speak of the centuries of anti-semitism culminating in the 'holocaust' of the Nazis. Lastly they detail the more recent antagonism of the Arab world. By contrast, the Palestinians prefer to emphasise the Arab presence in Palestine since the seventh century, the importance of Jerusalem as the second holy city of Islam, the dispossession of thousands of Palestinians and their life in refugee camps, and the Jewish settlement in the occupied territories. All these things are, in essence, undeniable historical facts, though partisans of one side or the other will passionately argue their relative relevance or their accuracy in detail. The point is that people live, die and kill for reasons like these. History kills!

Of course it would be naïve to suggest that this is the whole story. Urban deprivation, poverty, family antagonism, the wish for power over others and all sorts of other factors help create the gunman or woman, the chauvinist politician, the violent racist or the patriot. But the *justification* is nearly always rooted in history.

This is not in the least surprising when one considers the fact that the ability to accumulate and communicate information is one of the main abilities that distinguish us from other animals. Culture and civilisation are based on the fact that each human being does not have to relearn by experience all that others before have learned but can call on the collective experience, the racial memory of our ancestors. Some of this inherited experience is of a purely practical nature. We do not need a justification for using the wheel: once invented, its usefulness ensures its survival. But the complex patterns of social and economic life which characterise human culture need reinforcement. Societies are fragile things; they only work if most of their members play by the rules.

Societies persuade people to play by the rules partly by imposing sanctions on those who do not, but most of the time this is not necessary. As children we internalise the behaviour patterns of our society so that they become part of our identity. When children ask why 'we' do things in a certain way the answer is often a story. This is the case particularly when 'we' are being contrasted with 'them'. A Moslem child learns why he or she has to learn the Koran, when others are playing, in terms of a proud Islamic heritage. Others learn to distrust or hate members of another class or religion through the medium of family stories. All of us have a picture of our own identity that is coloured by our origins and the baggage of historical imagery they carry.

So, if history is a powerful force keeping us to the ways of our ancestors, how is it that things change at all?

The answer to this question is that history is not an immutable monolith, but, sometimes at least, a very plastic substance. In saying this I am not suggesting that history is fiction, though sometimes it comes close to being just that, but rather that each group or generation selects elements from the vast storeroom of the past to construct the foundation they need.

Sometimes this is a conscious process, as in Stalin's Russia where history books and records were rewritten and altered regularly to accommodate changes in the hierarchy. More often it is merely a case of redirected interest, and a reassessment of the importance of events or whole classes of information. This century has witnessed a surge of interest in social history, and the lives of ordinary people in the past, which reflects the growth of individualism. However, politicians, in particular, can and regularly do use history to illustrate their arguments and give them power.

The phrase 'Victorian values' was used on several occasions during the Thatcher administration in the context of the family and community care to imply self-reliance, discipline, private charitable work etc.

We should ask ourselves why modern social policy should be deliberately associated with life in a former age. The answer lies in the theory of *cause* and *effect*. The idea is that the Victorians did x and Victorian society was like y: therefore x *contributed to* y. I suspect that the image of Victorian society of which the politicians in question wished to remind us involved prosperity, industrial supremacy and the Empire. We are left with the inference that if only we were more like the Victorians in one way, we would be more like them in others.

There is nothing sinister about this; we *can* learn from the past, but we need not be tied to one interpretation of it. We can examine for ourselves what community care was like in Victorian Britain by looking at the *evidence*. This evidence may be found in documents, in objects, in buildings, in history books, in novels, in pictures and in the memories of those who lived in the period. As always in history we would find more than one point of view. A historian who wished to oppose the image of Victorian society as the heyday of the disciplined paternalistic family might care to mention the huge incidence of prostitution, illegitimacy, infant mortality and indigence. The evidence for this might be found in workhouse records, in the findings of commissions of enquiry, in novels or in the proto-sociological work of Mayhew. Often the sort of answers that historians wish to find influence the sorts of evidence they select to look at, or the interpretation that they put on it.

We should not lose sight of the fact, however, that history is not, as one of Voltaire's characters said 'no more than accepted fiction'. History derives its power and its strength as a justification for present action from the fact that we perceive it as *true*. Historians are rarely disinterested enquirers but they recognise that without the evidence their ideas mean nothing.

History in the primary school

In the period leading up to the publication of the National Curriculum statutory orders for history, an acrimonious debate raged as to what the emphasis of school history should be. One party argued for an 'active' learning approach, where children were introduced to the use of historical evidence at an early stage and where 'points of view', debate, role play and interpretation were prominent features. Their opponents advocated a much more factual content to lessons. Before we look at what was finally decided, and who, if anyone, won; we should look at the pros and cons of these approaches. We shall examine first the latter view.

There are really two prongs to the argument, a positive and a negative one. On the one hand there are reasons for a factual school history, on the other reasons against an investigative one.

The first of the 'positive reasons' is that history, unlike, for instance, philosophy or literature, is a factually based subject and that one needs a significant base of factual knowledge to work on before one can start to analyse it. Historians work on a very large canvas. Cause and effect may be said to work over hundreds of years; history is a continuous process and an understanding of its broad sweep is necessary to contextualise evidence which usually relates to one tiny corner of it. So, the argument is, schoolchildren should concentrate on getting the general picture into their heads.

It is not disputed by the proponents of this argument that even general pictures vary with viewpoint, but it is felt that there is a British national view of history which British children should learn. This point deserves, I think, to be taken very seriously.

If one examines school history books from the first half of this century, one does find a fairly unified picture. Infant histories were mostly concerned with telling a series of stories, 'Caractacus and the Roman Emperor', 'How King Alfred burnt the cakes', 'Hereward the Wake', 'Bruce and the spider' etc., which often had the character of moral parables. As the child grew older a more chronological and continuous story emerged; 'The ancient Britons', 'Julius Ceasar and the Romans', 'Hengist and Horsa and the Saxons', 'King Alfred and the English', 'The Battle of Hastings', 'King Richard the Lion Heart', etc., the emphasis being on famous men, usually kings, and battles, with the odd chapter of 'scene setting' detail on, for instance 'London before the Great Fire'.

More recent history was generally left until the secondary years which also featured a great deal of politics: 'The Great Reform Act of 1832', 'The Repeal of the Corn Laws', 'The Treaty of Vienna'. Books at this level are often arranged with sub-headings like the above in bold type on the left of the page and a few paragraphs of explanation under them. This facilitated the use of the book for its purpose of 'rote learning' the contents for an examination.

During the early part of this century, then, history in schools was learned as the story of how Britain became great, the stories of great men were given as exemplars of the formation of the British character, and the whole was intended to produce pride in the British identity. In doing this it had considerable success, and there can be little doubt that national pride was higher then than now. To gauge the conscious use made of history in this, we have only to look at the resources put into the production of historical films like *Henry V* during the Second World War.

Most people would, I think, agree that a certain amount of pride in one's national culture and identity is a very good thing (provided of course that it does not develop into contempt for other people's). I think that they would also accept that it is desirable for our children to gain a broad outline of the development of the British nation. The problem might be, and in the context of the National Curriculum has been, to reach agreement as to which particular historical facts should go into this National Story. For better or for worse the Britain of today is a very different place from that of the pre-war years and we need different elements from our past to help us understand it.

Let us take, for instance, the question of 'women's history'. Amongst the hordes of 'famous people' mentioned in my collection of about thirty pre-war history books I can find only twelve women. They are: Boadicea, Lady Godiva, Queen Matilda, Joan of Arc, Queen Elizabeth, Mary Queen of Scots, Queen Mary Tudor, Queen Anne, Queen Victoria, Florence Nightingale, Grace Darling and Marie Curie. Of these five were reigning monarchs who could not therefore be left out. This does not appear to give much weight to the contribution of the female half of the population to the development of the British nation. Note that it is not a question of whether there *is* any 'women's history': women were there therefore they have a story. It is rather a matter of whether we choose to look for it. There is no doubt that the view that women's lives may be subsumed into those of men is no longer acceptable in our society, so our national story must change.

Another major change in British society since the last war is its increasing heterogeneousness. Of course, Britain has always been a very diverse nation, containing a wide variety of ethnic, religious and class groupings. But its diversity is now much more visible, partly because the minority groups are now much greater in numbers, and partly because many are of non-European origin. Many Jewish or Italian immigrants in the early years of the century avoided discrimination by anglicising their names and accents, but this is not possible if you are black. Our nation is now very clearly a multi-cultural one with a common heritage that draws from half of the world. As Professor Stuart Hall, amongst others, has cogently argued 'Black History' is not just for black children, it is part of the story of modern Britain, and we all need it if we are to find our identity as a people.

There is a case to be made for many other elements not present in traditional British history to be included in our new national story.

Unfortunately there would never be time to teach them all in schools. The curriculum is already, in the eyes of most teachers, vastly overloaded, and a considerable amount of selection must take place. Equally unfortunately Margaret Thatcher's opinion, voiced in parliament, that there were certain 'landmarks' in British history that we could all agree about, has proved incorrect. Experts consulted by the working party for history, and those who offered unsolicited advice, disagreed, and still disagree vehemently about what should go in and what stay out. There is also a substantial body of opinion that feels that it is not the place of the government to dictate content at all, and that this decision should be left to the school or to the individual teacher.

To sum up, then, if you have a 'fact-based' history, we have a real problem deciding which facts, and who chooses them.

The negative reason against the active learning approach to primary history, as given by the so-called 'right wing' in the history debate, is that young children are held to be incapable of using evidence in a useful manner. Such work, it is argued, takes a great deal of experience, skill and knowledge; and is properly left to the university years. I feel that this argument shows little understanding of the nature and purpose of primary education. After all, nobody expects a primary school science class to make major discoveries in nuclear physics, yet we feel it our duty to teach the pupils scientific method, and expect them to carry out experiments. As I hope will be quite clear in the following chapters the skills required for historical research in the primary school are life-skills: observation, discrimination, the weighing of points of view, logic and above all the ability to recognise our common humanity manifested in the innumerable ways of living of which human beings are capable.

Probably no factor has had a more profound effect on post-war society, at least in the 'first and second worlds', than the all-pervasiveness of modern communications. In 1938 it was possible for Neville Chamberlain to refer to Hitler's invasion of Czechoslovakia as 'a quarrel in a far-away country between people of whom we know nothing'. Such a statement would be inconceivable today. Whilst I would not suggest that we are now all internationalists, the television brought images of Czechoslovakia and Vaclav Havel into all our living rooms during the recent collapse of the communist regime in that country. In the attempted right-wing coup in the Soviet Union of August 1991, President Gorbachev, beleaguered in the Crimea, kept up with the news by listening to the BBC World Service. We are deluged by images, stories and points of view from around the world.

It is a common complaint that our media are biased. During the Falklands War and the war with Iraq many felt that the anti-war arguments were not given sufficient weight in the newspapers and on TV. But it is an undeniable fact that such opinions were available nationally. The so-called 'quality press' and television documentaries did give some space to alternative points of view. If these points of view had no impact it must mean either that they were weighed and rejected by the mass of the population, or that the mass of the population were not sufficiently educated in looking for and processing such information. Whatever one's views on this, it is clear (to me anyway) that a democratic country in the modern world should be teaching its future citizens to form their opinions by evaluating the evidence and opinions available. There is no better way of learning these skills than in the critical study of history.

The last, but by no means the least important argument for an investigative approach to primary history is that most children find it much more enjoyable and challenging than just learning facts. The proof of this pudding is in the eating.

The statutory orders for history

I do not propose to attempt here a detailed analysis of the statutory orders for history. For one thing they are reasonably clear in themselves; for another, it has already been proved that the National Curriculum is not unchangeable, it has already been revised and is quite likely to be revised again. However, certain points should be noted in the light of the preceding debate.

The writers of the document have used the standard National Curriculum structure of Attainment Targets (ATs) and Programmes of Study to try to satisfy, to some extent, both parties in the debate (naturally enough, with limited success). The ATs lay down a framework of historical skills and concepts. These should be progressively applied through the Programmes of Study, which contain prescribed content. At Key Stage 2 this content is delivered through Study Units (SUs). In simple terms the SUs in the Programme tell you what material to work on, and the ATs tell you what a child at a particular level should be able to do with the material.

The writers resisted considerable pressure to include a list of facts in the ATs which every child should know, and the prescribed content of the SUs is limited to single A4 pages of quite loose guidelines. The appended Non-Statutory Guidelines go into rather more detail on suggested ways of satisfying the requirements.

History and the non-historian teacher

The publication of the statutory orders for history have been met with widespread trepidation by classroom teachers. In some cases this is due to the sheer volume of material that the primary school teacher is expected to get through, and is, I feel, justified. In other cases, however, two other reasons are given. Either the teacher feels that they just do not know enough history themselves or they disliked history during their own schooldays, and doubt their ability to be enthusiastic about it.

The latter reason is often given by those who were taught by traditional methods, learning facts. People who experienced this emphasis usually ended up either loving history or hating it. Those who loved it usually did so because they liked *the stories*, and we should never forget that storytelling is an indispensable part of history teaching. Those who hated it, however, did so because they found it irrelevant and boring. The solution, for both teacher and pupil is to make history relevant and interesting. My experience is that the investigative and skill-based methods outlined in this book do just that.

For many younger teachers the problem is that they have been taught so little history when at school themselves. Her Majesty's Inspectorate's report, *The Teaching and Learning of History and Geography* (1989), was damning about the amount and standard of history taught during the 1980s. It found that:

> In two out of three infant classes history received little or no attention. The situation was slightly better in junior-aged classes but even so history was underemphasised or not taught in half the sample schools at the time of inspection. (p.8)

The HMI report further found that what history there was tended to be either based on television programmes, which were often not followed up, or was a fortuitous spin-off from a 'topic' centred in another area of the curriculum.

'The topic' was at the centre of primary school teaching throughout the 1970s and 1980s, and it remains so in many schools today. In emphasising the connections between areas of knowledge, it provided a meaningful focus for the curriculum. But there is no doubt that, as the HMI report found, continuity and progression in individual disciplines were sometimes left behind in the enthusiasm for holism. History was not often selected as a central theme for the topic and therefore it tended to get tacked on, with little thought given to the development of historical concepts or knowledge.

One should not gain the impression from this that primary school history was completely dormant in the second half of this century. Much good work was done, and writers like Joan Blyth, John Fines, John West and many others pioneered the sorts of methods that are now being advocated. But the work went on only in certain schools, and within those schools it often only happened in the class of one teacher who had a personal enthusiasm for the subject. The strength of the National Curriculum is that it attempts to ensure that all children will get the benefit of the work of the pioneers.

Our problem is how best to provide all primary school teachers with an enthusiasm for history. As to the way of doing this, I differ from some prominent commentators. It has been suggested that the Programmes of Study form the best 'way in' for the non-specialist. I feel that asking teachers to impart a series of presented facts, which they are often unsure about themselves, is not the best way to boost confidence. On the other hand, the methodology of investigative history, once understood, is usually recognised as a familiar friend by good teachers, and it is often in the methodology that parallels and cross-curricular connections can be made. Similarly the main concepts of chronology, continuity, change, cause and effect, evidence etc. are ideas that professional teachers can grasp and use their skills and ingenuity to deliver. In this book, then, we will examine the *methods of dealing with primary evidence*, using examples from the prescribed content given in the National Curriculum for history.

Further reading

National Curriculum Council (1991) *History in the National Curriculum* (statutory orders and non-statutory guidelines). London: Department of Education and Science.

HMI (1989) *The Teaching and Learning of History and Geography*. London: Department of Education and Science.

Carr, E.H. (1987) *What is History?* Harmondsworth: Penguin (second edition).

Gardiner, J. (ed.) (1990) *The History Debate*. London: Collins & Brown.

CHAPTER 2
How to Look at Artefacts

The statutory orders for history state that in both Key Stages 1 and 2 'pupils should have opportunities to learn about the past from a range of sources, including . . . artefacts'. One of the main ways in which anthropologists define human beings is by their ability to make and use artefacts. Artefacts are elements of the natural world modified to serve technological and/or aesthetic purposes, and it is a basic human characteristic to make them. We are not unique in this ability: birds make nests and ants make anthills. But they make them instinctively, without needing to plan or learn. Chimpanzees have been recorded as quite extensive tool users, some groups having a repertoire of about a dozen types from nut crackers to termite catching rods; but their productions are extremely basic compared to the simplest Stone Age hand axe.

Most anthropologists now believe that modern human beings originated in Africa and first entered Europe about 36,000 years ago; and there is evidence that other species who were very like modern humans in their bone structure and brain size (or at least more like humans than apes) were here long before that, maybe 400,000 years ago. Writing was first introduced to Britain just before the Romans got here, only about 2,000 years ago. This means that for by far the greatest part of the human occupation of this country the only evidence we have is bones and artefacts. The bones tell us about physical characteristics, but the artefacts provide the only clues as to how people lived.

Even when we enter the era of the written word there are massive gaps in the documentary record. Until very recently writing was the preserve of the rich, the establishment and of men rather than women. Artefacts on the other hand permeate all classes and types. All known human societies use vast numbers of objects in every area of their lives. Objects are involved in nearly all our activities and if they could speak they could tell more of our secrets than any of our friends. The problem is to make them speak. *Artefacts should not be seen as illustrations to the text of history, but as a text in themselves, a text that can tell us things that we can learn nowhere else.*

I would suggest that there are at least two stages which are necessary to the successful use of artefacts in the classroom. First the child (and the teacher) must learn something of the theory of 'material culture'. We are used to the idea that documents contain information, but 'reading' objects seems unfamiliar. In fact it is something we do all the time; but, because the act is usually unconscious, we need to find out how we do it and establish a method. The child also needs some knowledge of the process of archaeology, since we learn infinitely more from objects in their archaeological context than we can from the same objects in isolation. Secondly, there is the application of evidence gained from artefacts in the study of a historical period. For each study unit, the child must learn how to evaluate different forms of evidence and how to fit them together to build up an accurate picture of the time in question.

Method

There is nothing more important in the study of artefacts than establishing a systematic and coherent method for children's investigations. Too often such work can turn into a random guessing game. Of course some guesswork will be necessary, but it should take the form of reasoned hypotheses which develop after as many facts as possible have been established.

Often the best approach to reading unfamiliar objects is to compare and contrast them with familiar ones. Children need a point of reference within their own experience on which to base any new learning. An activity that works well is to collect a small number of artefacts from widely different periods, including one modern item, the task being to sequence them into a 'timeline'.

In my experience it is very important to insist upon *no* guesses at the beginning of the game, the reason being that once children have made a guess it is often very difficult to shift them from it even in the face of a great deal of evidence. If you are not careful it becomes a case of proving one another wrong rather than a shared exercise in logical investigation.

At the start of the activity the only object the children are sure of is the modern one. As an example of a modern artefact I often use a felt tip marker. The first question to be addressed is 'how do we know that this is new?' Children give answers like:

'It's made of plastic.'

'It's still shiny.'
'It's just like the ones we use every day.'
'It still works.'
'It's bright red.'
'It's got modern writing on it.'

The trick is to organise such responses into categories of information that will help us analyse any object. I often use the board to record children's answers, allocating each to a column representing a particular category of evidence. I give the columns the following headings:

TECHNOLOGY OF THE OBJECT
(What it is made of and how it is made)
'It's made of plastic.'

CONDITION OF THE OBJECT
'It's still shiny.'
'It still works.'

STYLE OF THE OBJECT
'It's just like the ones we use every day.'

INSCRIPTIONS
'It's got modern writing on it.'

The comment 'It's bright red' could quite properly be classified as evidence of condition, but it sometimes comes up because children think that bright colours did not exist in the past. I have even found children who, having seen old black and white photographs, conclude that the world was monochrome until recently! It is a good idea to find colour pictures of, for instance, a mural from Pompeii, to disabuse them of this idea.

It will be noted that we have not yet looked at the use of the object at all. This is because the above information is all visible and empirically verifiable, whereas we will probably have to guess at the function. An idea which may be introduced early in the discussion will be that most objects have a social function as well as a practical one. Children will readily understand what is meant by this if they are asked what a Porsche sports car is for. Clearly the practical function of a Porsche is to transport someone from A to B, but we all understand that anyone buying a Porsche does so mainly to tell the world certain things about himself. In a less obvious way we all draw all sorts of conclusions about people from their dress, their homes and all the objects that people surround themselves with from choice or necessity.

This is especially true in our consumer society, but objects have always formed a part of human interactions and communication, and many of the most interesting things to be learned from them are in this sphere.

I therefore suggest a programme of investigation, as summarised in Figure 2.1.

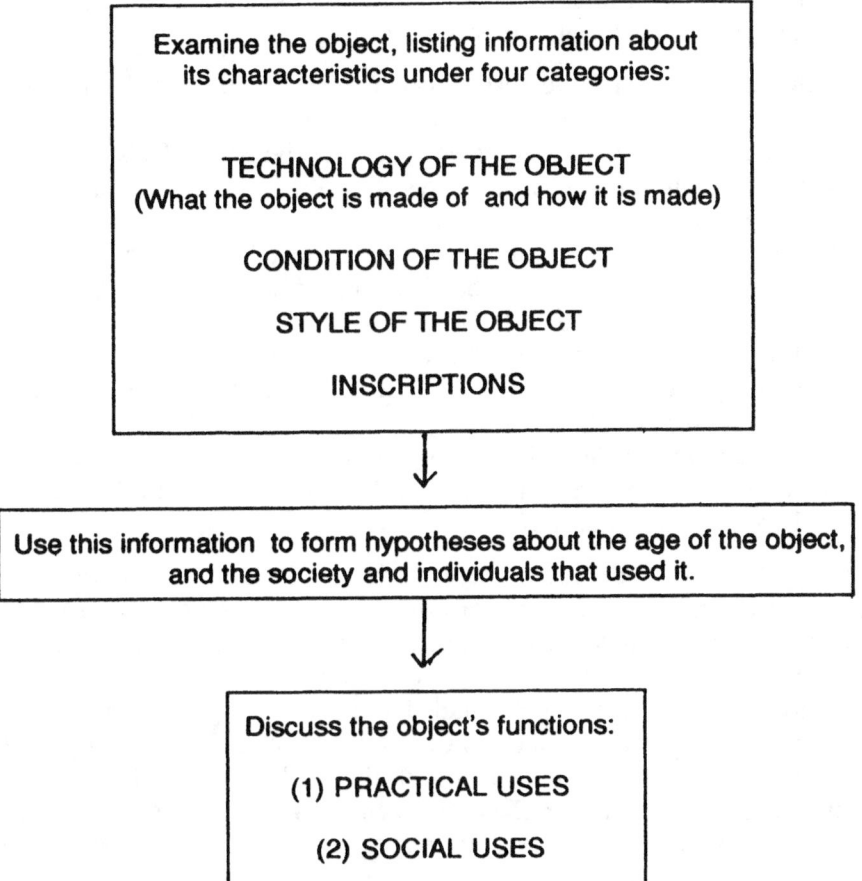

Figure 2.1 Programme of investigation for the analysis of artefacts

We can now embark upon the investigation into an unfamiliar object. If children are to engage effectively in this programme they will need guidance. Their observations are usually very acute, but they will need help to organise these observations in a logical way. Here are some suggestions on how to handle each category of information.

Technology of the object (what it's made of and how it's made)

Do not assume that children or adults will be able to recognise materials unaided. They must be taught to do so (the National Curriculum orders for science require that they should be). It is a good idea to have a set of similar objects made of different materials: drinking cups, for instance, can be found made of plastic, enamel, tin, china, paper, horn and wood. Children can be encouraged to apply various tests to find their different characteristics:

> Temperature – (a good test to do first as handling will affect it). Which material feels warmest/coolest?
> Texture – which words describe best how the object feels?
> Weight – which object feels heaviest? (Objects of comparable size must be used.)
> Sound – what sort of sound does the material make when tapped lightly with a pencil? (Hold the object up off any resonating surface while carrying out this test.)
> Colour – what colour is the object? Is the colour natural or artificial?
> Flexibility/rigidity – is the object soft, hard, fragile, strong, malleable? (Test gently!)
> Cross-section – if the object is chipped or broken, can you see what the inner fabric of the material is like? Is it the same right through or is there an outer coating?

Useful links can be made here with the Attainment Targets in geography and science, the statutory orders for which require that children should know the origin of raw materials in the environment and have some idea of how they are extracted.

Knowing what something is made from can be helpful in finding out about an object or the society that used it, but often finding out how it was made is even more useful. Materials can be processed in a finite number of ways which reflect the technological abilities and commercial or aesthetic requirements of the makers and users. Here are some examples.

Clay

> Ceramic objects can be made by three basic methods:
> 1. *By hand.* This includes finger pots, coil pots, slab pots. Hand manufacture can be recognised by lack of symmetry, thick construction, finger marks in the clay, odd shapes.
> 2. *On a wheel.* These will be circular, fine in construction, flat-based, often showing the undulating marks of throwing.

3. *Moulded.* Often a join between two moulded halves (which may or may not be exactly the same) can be seen. The object may have decoration in low relief, this is easy to produce on moulded objects, by cutting the pattern into the mould. Moulded ceramics often have rather a 'clean' finish.

Something can also be deduced about the firing process by simple examination. For instance, before the kiln was introduced into Britain by the Romans, pots were fired in a simple 'bonfire'. You can recognise them by their thick fabric, by 'inclusions' (pieces of flint, grains, feathers or other material mixed into the clay which can be seen in the cross section of a shard), or sometimes by uneven colour or burnt sections.

Apart from evidence about date, which comes from the complexity of the manufacturing process, other simple deductions can be made. If a pot was clearly made in a mould then obviously the potter intended to make a lot of similar pots. That implies that he/she was a specialist making for some sort of market. It also implies that the pot originated in a society with towns (centres where goods can be exchanged), reasonable transport, maybe money.

Metals

The first thing to do is to attempt to identify the metal. Archaeologists often use the colour of any corrosion. Common ones are:

BROWN. Iron oxide, commonly known as rust.
GREEN TO TURQUOISE. Copper oxide. The object may be copper or a copper alloy such as bronze (copper and tin), or brass (copper and zinc).
BLACK. Both silver and pure tin corrode black but tin tends to look greyer.
WHITE. Lead goes a dusty white, aluminium a 'crusty' white. You can easily tell the difference by the weight.

Once you have identified the metal there are several ways of working it:

1. *Forging.* This means that the object has been heated on the forge and hammered into shape. The object may be slightly asymmetrical or show hammer marks, but this depends on the skill of the smith and on the use of the object.
2. *Hammering.* Bowls are sometimes hammered out when cold, from softer metals like copper. You can see the whole surface of the bowl covered with little dents.

3. *Casting*. This means that the object is made in a mould, often showing seams or casting marks.
4. *Rolling*. This is an industrial process to make sheets of metal that are often then bent into shape.

Casting and forging are very ancient techniques (you can see Bronze Age moulds in many museums), whereas rolling is much more modern.

Wood

To identify which wood an artefact is made of you will need either a reference book, of which there are many, or even a pack of wood veneers. The latter are produced for educational use or by specialist timber merchants (get current addresses from woodworking magazines in your stationers). Having identified the wood, a basic question is whether it is a native or imported timber. Objects made by country craftsmen for everyday use were made from common local wood like oak, beech, ash. In the eighteenth century highly figured woods like walnut became popular for expensive furniture. This had to be imported, which says something about transport and communications. Many Victorian objects are made from exotic hardwoods like mahogany and blackwood, while in the late Victorian period cheap imported 'deal' or pinewood took over from the native woods for making such things as kitchen tables or dressers. Earlier pine objects were made from wood which grew slowly: it is harder and the annular rings are close together, whereas modern pine is forced up quickly and is softer with the rings further apart.

Many books have been written about the craft of the woodworker and it would be vain to try to summarise such a vast subject. An area of particular interest is the use of different woods with different properties for different purposes. Leslie Alcock's *Sweet Track to Glastonbury* details how craftsmen of the New Stone Age used a combination of woods to construct a causeway across the Somerset Levels 6,000 years ago. Sturt's *The Wheelwright's Shop* shows Edwardian craftsmen applying the same skill and knowledge to the making of wagons and wheels. Many museums of rural life have sections and materials on woodworking techniques.

Work on the technology of the object can become as complex as you want it to or you have the knowledge for. An excellent textbook on early techniques is Hodges (1989) *Artifacts* published by Duckworth. The important message to give to children is that every object started life as a piece of nature which has been moulded and processed by another human being. Finding out how they did it brings us much closer to them and their lives.

Condition of the object

It is very difficult to give an accurate estimate of an object's age purely by its condition. It obviously depends very much on how it has been looked after or in what circumstances it has been preserved. Most materials, however, deteriorate to a greater or lesser extent over time. Children can experiment to find out how different materials behave by burying a range of objects for several weeks and seeing how they change. The process can be accelerated by watering them liberally every day.

Organic materials

These include anything that was once alive e.g. wood, leather, straw, cotton. All organic materials *rot*. *This means that they are attacked by fungi or bacteria and biodegrade.* For this reason objects made of these things are rarely found in archaeology. They only survive in very special conditions which do not allow the fungi or bacteria to work: in very dry conditions like deserts, in peat bogs (which are very acidic), sometimes in muddy river banks or in ice. Two very exciting examples to look at are the Lindow bog man 'Peat Marsh', in the British Museum, and the recently discovered 'Ice Man' found on the Italian-Austrian border.

Metals

All metals found in archaeology *corrode* with the exception of gold, which perhaps explains its universal fascination. Some metals corrode much more quickly and more completely than others. Iron can corrode away to a brown stain in the earth in as little as one hundred years in some conditions.

Ceramics

Well-fired pottery undergoes a change in its crystalline structure, which makes the fabric itself fairly indestructible (though of course the pot breaks quite easily). In the British Museum there is 3,000-year-old pottery that looks as if it could have been made yesterday. It is often better to ask the children if the object being studied looks as if it has been buried for a long time. Look for earth in inaccessible crannies. If it is unglazed it might have patchy discoloration due to salts washed through the soil.

Signs of wear on an object may give a clue to its use. Often you can tell how a much used wooden object was held by discoloration. Objects like a washing dolly may show evidence that some parts were used in water because they have a washed out appearance and open grain. Even with a stone implement, a close look with a magnifying glass may reveal the 'business end' and thus help to show its use.

If an object is broken or incomplete then it is important to try to reconstruct its original appearance. This involves careful drawing of the existing object, careful observation of it to find where there are missing parts, and tracing curves or looking for asymmetry to guess what they looked like. You can break modern pottery and give a shard to the children to work on. Photograph it before you break it, or retain a similar unbroken example, so that the children's reconstructional drawings can be checked against it.

Style of the object

In 'real' archaeology style is often the main criterion for dating an object. Archaeologists get to know which things belong to which period. Unfortunately this requires one to have a library of styles in one's head with which to compare. Children cannot be expected to have this information automatically; they have to build it up as they get a mental picture of different times in history. One way around this is to have a variety of pictures available which show, for instance, a Roman banquet, a medieval one, or a Victorian dinner party. Children examining a pot can say which picture it belongs in by looking at shapes, colours and textures. I have found children to be surprisingly good at this. Many large museums produce postcard-sized reconstructions suitable for this purpose, and some posters are in the catalogues of major educational chart distributors. Shire Publications publish a large number of booklets containing photographs of just about every sort of museum object.

We should not forget that styles are often reused. In 1990 Edwardian button boots were fashionable for women but they can be easily distinguished from the 1910 originals by their *technology* (plastic soles instead of leather ones and the edge of the leather left rough instead of being turned over as in a hem). Also their *condition* may be different: the old leather may be hard and cracked, but this will depend on how they have been kept.

Inscriptions

Inscriptions on objects can give all sorts of information apart from a date, which is always worth looking for.

Manufacturers' names

If the company which made the object is still in business then they will be pleased to give information. I once had to identify a curious object made of stainless steel that appeared to be a clamp of some sort, the only clue being the name 'JAQUES' stamped on it. Directory Enquiries told me that there was a sports equipment firm of that name in London. I rang them and asked to speak to somebody who had been in the company a long time. A very pleasant gentleman came on to the line and I described my object. He asked me to measure the distance between its jaws. When I told him the answer he knew immediately: 'It's for correcting the size of croquet hoops' he said. Not everyone would have known that!

Patent numbers

Patented designs are registered at the Patents Office with the year the patent was granted. Of course many designs stay in use for long periods after that.

Country of origin

This can tell us something of trade and communications in the past.

Handwritten inscriptions

These can show different styles of handwriting or popular first names for a period. A personal name can forge a powerful link in our minds with the original owner.

Other sorts of information can yield clues if you refer to an expert for the particular type of object. For instance, if you have a military badge with a number on it then the Imperial War Museum will tell you about the regiment which wore it.

As a general rule one should not hesitate to consult museums. Nearly all of them have an identification service which may be on the spot, or you may be asked to leave the object with them for a short od. Letters of enquiry from children will receive courteous and archaeology, but it is better to go to a specialist for more unusual enquiries, such as The Museum of Mankind for something that looks 'tribal' or The National Maritime Museum for something connected to the sea.

Practical function

If the above process of enquiry has been pursued rigorously, it is very likely that ideas about practical function will have emerged by now. If the object is outside modern experience, such as a stone tool, it may help to remember that it was designed to be used by human beings just like us. If it feels awkward in your hand then you are probably holding it wrongly. If the blade looks too blunt to cut then maybe it was designed to scrape. Has it got handles? Does it stand up by itself? Is it decorative?

Social function

This is the most difficult thing to tell, especially if you do not know anything about the society that produced the object. The key idea to bear in mind is *status*. If an object is more decorative, made of a more valuable material, or has more hours of work invested in its manufacture than its practical function requires, then it was probably intended to attract status to its owner. Silver-inlaid needlework scissors were made to show that the owner was a lady not a seamstress. A highly polished stone axe from the New Stone Age must have taken days to make, and could not have worked much better than a simple roughly finished one that took ten minutes, so it must have been considered valuable in itself, and was not created just for its utility. A twist may be added when an object is 'pretending to be what it is not'. Modern plastic jewellery, for instance, is sometimes painted to look like gold, while some Roman pottery is burnished to look like bronze. In both cases a low-status object is trying to look like a high-status one, implying that the objects belong to a society where people are judged by what they own, and one in which social aspiration can be expressed through acquiring things. This shows that social mobility in that society was possible, since it would not be worth aspiring if status was firmly fixed by birth.

In the classroom

Clearly museums are the key environment for studying artefacts from particular periods, not least because they are the only place you will find many of them. The necessity of visiting a museum depends also on which study unit is being pursued. It is easy enough to find Victorian or twentieth-century objects yourself but older things are much more difficult. It is important that children work with artefacts in the classroom as well as the museum, however – and as an on-going process not just as a 'one-off' lesson. This is because children need time and help to learn to 'read' objects, just as they need time and help to learn to read books. 'Reading' objects means learning the basic principles of examining an artefact and deducing information about the past. There are a number of well-tried activities for developing these skills outlined in English Heritage's *Teacher's Guide to Learning from Objects* and it would be redundant to repeat them here. Also I feel that it is important that the purpose of such activities is well understood first by the teacher, who can then develop his or her own variations in a developing programme.

Where to find objects

To teach the theory of reading objects you need to build up a collection of small non-valuable artefacts spanning as long a time period as possible. This cannot be done all at once and it involves developing an eye for an object with good teaching properties. Here are some useful sources; see what you can find in:

1. The houses of older members of your own family. If my own family is anything to judge by, they will be only too pleased to contribute to children's learning about the past. Look for anything Victorian, Edwardian, wartime or even objects from the 1960s. Things made of different materials from modern versions, things used in processes now done by machines (kitchen and laundry equipment work well), clothing (children love old-fashioned underwear!), gas masks and ration books, old toys are all very useful.
2. Car boot sales and junk shops yield the same sort of material, but avoid anyone with claims to be an antique dealer as they will have prices to match their pretensions.
3. Sending a letter home to your pupils' parents for material often brings fascinating results, though usually the objects will only be loaned. It might be worth keeping a register of such sources for future use.
4. An appeal in the local newspaper for objects for the school museum can often reap rewards.
5. Dig your garden! Shards of Victorian pottery etc. come up in many backyards.

6. Get permission from a farmer to 'walk' newly ploughed fields. In this way I have found flint tools and clay pipes.
7. If there is an archaeological dig happening anywhere near you (the local museum will know), go and have a word with the site director. Material useful to you may be coming off above the level in which they are interested and thus be on the spoil heap. On some digs less important material such as common pottery shards will not be preserved after they have been planned and noted, so the archaeologists may be willing to give you some.
8. Above all, let everyone know you are interested in 'old things'. Many of my most interesting pieces were gifts.

Further reading

Durbin, G. *et al.* (1989) *Teachers Guide to Learning from Objects.* London: English Heritage.
Edlin, H. (1977) *What Wood is That.* London: Stobart.
Hodges, H. (1989) *Artifacts.* London: Duckworth.
West, J. (1990) *The Classroom Museum.* Huntingdon: Elm Publications.

CHAPTER 3
Artefacts in Context

The sort of activity outlined in the previous chapter is something like the process gone through by a museum curator who is trying to classify an unidentified object. The real 'meat' of information about people's lives in the past, however, comes from putting the objects in their context and finding out how they interact. To an archaeologist, *where* you find an artefact is as important as what it is. In this chapter we will look at the basic principles of archaeology and also at how assemblages of objects may be used to support the study of a particular period.

Archaeologists dig in the ground to find objects and other evidence (pollen grains, pieces of charcoal, post holes, fire marks etc.) that show what life was like in the past. The first question that must be answered is how the material got into the ground in the first place. This may seem obvious to adults, but to young children it is not.

With Key Stage 1 classes a simple role play is often effective. If you have already done some work with artefacts and told stories set in widely different periods as prescribed in the National Curriculum, then those earlier activities can be used as a basis for the role play. If you cannot get real artefacts, then use replicas (making sure that the children know that they are such). A flint tool can be made (see Chapter 5), and replica 'Roman' lamps are available quite cheaply at museums as are coins of various eras, while shards of pottery, modern or older are not difficult to find.

Role play

The role play may be undertaken with groups or as a class. It may be based closely on stories told beforehand or be original. The important thing is that the children should use the information that they have about the period of each object to tell a story about how it was lost or discarded. For instance:

> A woman in the Stone Age is frightened by wolves and drops her scraper as she runs away. She never came back to find it, and in the autumn the trees around

shed their leaves till it was hidden. In the winter it rained and snowed till the dead leaves went black and mushy and eventually turned into soil. After 2,000 winters you can imagine that a lot of leaves had fallen and the soil covering the scraper was quite thick.

Two thousand years later a Roman was coming home from market with a new lamp. It was a hot day and he was tired, so he stopped for a nap under a tree (he did not know that the scraper was buried underneath his feet). He slept longer than he intended, and when he woke up he hurried home, forgetting to pick up the lamp which he had put down on the ground. In the autumn . . . (the children can carry on the story to explain how each of your artefacts was lost).

The leaves falling can be simulated by newspaper. When you have finished the game the class can become archaeologists and dig down through the layers to find the objects. Use this opportunity to bring out the principle that those things near the surface must be newer than those below them. In this way you can show how there is a timeline going down into the soil.

The standard 'layer cake' diagram of a cross section of soil with the objects placed in it (Figure 3.1) can be drawn for the classroom wall.

What happens on a 'dig'

Archaeologists dig because they have reason to believe that something is below the surface. Maybe builders have already uncovered something, or aerial photographs have revealed interesting shapes in a field. Before anything else happens basic grid lines are marked out with a compass and stakes so that each stage of the dig can be carefully mapped and recorded. A key point will be chosen, and from this levels can be taken to find the relative depths of each find or stratum of soil.

Next the Site Director will choose where to dig the first *trench*. A trench is any one section of digging and it will have a number. The Director will lay out the trench so that it will give her the best idea of 'what is going on' underneath. For instance if aerial photos have revealed the shape of a building she may well decide to cut the trench straight across one wall.

The trench will be carefully aligned to the grid lines and marked with stakes and string. Then the turf is cut off (usually it is put aside so that it can be replaced later). Under the turf is the topsoil which is usually dark brown because it contains humus. Most of this can be shovelled off and again put aside on a *spoil heap*. Under the topsoil the archaeologist looks for the first level or *context*. This is signalled by a change in soil colour and harder packed earth.

The basic tool of archaeology is a small bricklayer's trowel made for

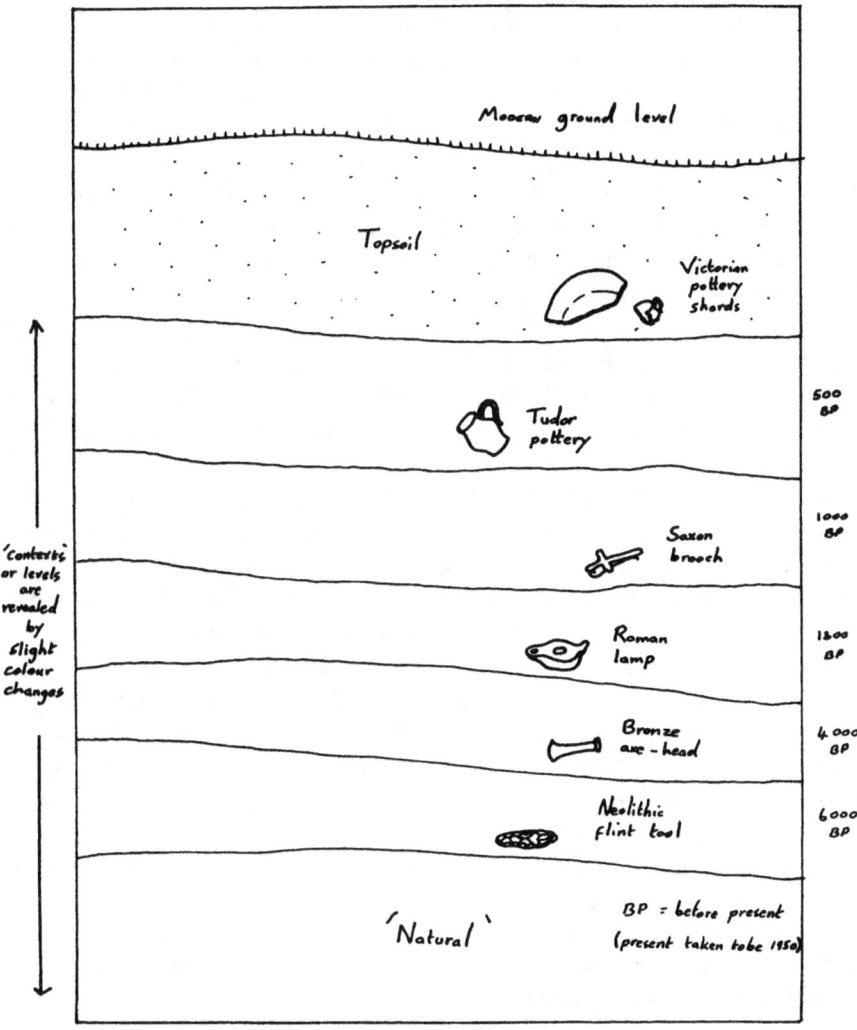

Figure 3.1 'Layer cake' diagram of archaeological levels

pointing up brickwork. Starting at one edge the archaeologist carefully scrapes off the remaining topsoil, cleaning the surface of the first *level* and looking very carefully for anything. The 'anything' may be small broken pieces of pottery, which would be very useful since she may recognise the style or technology involved and thus be able to date that level. It would then be likely that anything else found in that same coloured soil at that depth would be from the same period. Pieces of charcoal from house fires are common finds near human habitation: an expert can tell, from a big enough piece, what sort of tree it came from and therefore what the vegetation was like at that period. Organic substances, like charcoal, can also be carbon dated, though this is an expensive process and not undertaken lightly. If there is a circular patch of earth of a darker colour this may show where a post has rotted away, and the archaeologist will be on the lookout for more of them, maybe in a line or a big circle giving the shape of a house or a partition within a house. In stony areas of the country the earth may contain many rocks, and decisions must be made whether these form an ordered structure or are just randomly scattered.

Anything found is kept carefully in numbered bags with a note of which trench it was found in, in which context, and on which plan it will appear. A plastic label with the number of the find is stuck into the ground exactly where it was found. As each level is cleared, it is mapped with the use of a large grid consisting of a framework with strings stretched across it, placed over the trench and lined up with the side of it. Someone will then have to make a plan. Taking off her shoes so as not to trample the cleared context (or get caught in the strings), the archaeologist stands over each square of the grid and draws what is in it, including stones, 'find numbers', post holes etc.

If the archaeologist thinks that she has found a structure, she will extend the trench in the direction where she thinks the corner might be, for instance, or open a new trench in another strategic place. Or she may decide to go down to another level, which involves a lot more meticulous trowelling. The new level will again be signalled by a change in soil colour and/or texture.

Of course there are moments when people leap up in great excitement waving (carefully) a golden brooch in the air, but such moments are not really the point of the exercise, which is the systematic uncovering of every scrap of evidence and the recording of all of it for later interpretation.

Carbon dating

Many people have heard of carbon dating and they tend to think of it as a magical and foolproof way of finding out how old anything is. It is certainly a very useful technique, but it has its limitations. For a start it can only be used on organic substances (those that were once living, such as wood, leather or natural fabric). It works on bone marrow, but not on bone.

All such substances contain carbon, and the carbon contains a very small amount of radio-activity. When the plant or animal dies, the radio-activity begins to decay at a fixed rate. It never disappears completely, but just keeps halving its output for ever. This means that if, for instance, we find a piece of oak charcoal weighing one gramme in the ground, we can measure its radio-activity and compare it to that of a new piece of oak. Since we know the rate of decay, the difference in output will show us how long ago the wood was cut. However, the calculation is only accurate to around one hundred years each way, so the technique is only useful for dating very old things where a couple centuries makes no difference.

The other main drawback to carbon dating is the cost of the process. It can only be carried out in certain places with sophisticated equipment. In 1992 the cost for one date was around £,1000. Few archaeological digs have that sort of money to throw around.

Dendrochronology

Dendrochronology is another very accurate dating technique of which Key Stage 2 children can easily understand the principles. They also like the name! Most children know that trees can be dated after they have been cut down by counting the annular rings, because each of these signals a year's growth. If you look at a cross-section of wood you will see that the rings vary in width. This is because, due to varying weather conditions, the tree grows more in some years than in others. So, if you draw a radius from the bark to the heart of your section of tree trunk, you have another sort of timeline, recording the variations in summer weather from the time the tree started growing till the time it was cut down. If you now took a section from another tree of the same species grown in the same area you would find exactly the same pattern of thick and thin rings. Their size might be different, but the pattern of their relative sizes would be the same. If this tree was older than the first one then the timeline would extend further back.

In places where archaeologists find a lot of wood, such as Irish bogs, they have been able, with computers, to record the patterns of growth of oak trees for every year from the present, back to thousands of years ago. This means that if they find an object made of oak they can date the wood it was made from, absolutely, and thus date anything found with it.

Other sorts of scientific analysis

Probably the other most common forms of scientific analysis used on archaeological material are phosphate and pollen analysis.

Checks for phosphate levels in the soil tell you if an area has been used for keeping animals. Quite simply the animal droppings and urine contain high levels of phosphates which stay in the ground. For much of history farmhouses in Britain were used to shelter both humans and farm animals, often separated only by a partition (the body heat of the animals helped keep the house warm in winter). The distribution of phosphates in the soil show you which half of the house was for humans and which for animals.

Pollen is another substance valuable to archaeologists since it is fairly indestructible and remains in the soil to tell you about the surrounding flora at a particular period.

There are other complex processes that can help to date things by chemical means or by X-rays, but in general it is style and technology (as outlined in the previous chapter) and the association with other objects, in a particular context, that establish dates.

Work on archaeology with children

Probably the best way to teach children about archaeology and to engage their interest in it is to take them on a visit to a real dig. This is becoming an increasingly likely possibility as archaeologists are becoming more and more aware of the importance of public understanding and support for their work. There are many digs going on at any one time in the summer. Some will be high pressure 'rescue' digs which have a deadline before the builders move in, but many do allow school visits. These will be under strict supervision, not only because valuable evidence could easily be destroyed by a careless young foot, but also because sites are dangerous places with holes and piles of rubble about. Usually the visit would involve a guided tour and explanation together with a view of recent finds, though sometimes children may even be allowed to dig.

To find out about digs in your area either ask at the local museum or look up the County Archaeological Unit in the telephone directory. Go to the site yourself and speak to the Site Director. At the very least there may be a good vantage point from which your children could watch while you explain, having been briefed by the archaeologists.

A second sort of visit is to an ancient monument in your area. A hillfort or causewayed camp would do very well. Even in or near cities there are a surprising number of these. They are marked on standard Ordinance Survey maps but you might like to get *The Ordinance Survey Map of Ancient Britain* or consult Bord, J. and C. (1979) *A Guide to Ancient Sites in Britain* published by Paladin.

I have found it an interesting exercise to take the children 'cold', giving them no information beforehand of the accepted explanation of the site, only telling them that they are going to interpret some unusual evidence. I then ask a series of questions such as these:

1. Within this area, which features are natural and which human-made? How can you tell?
2. Is there any evidence how long ago the non-natural features were made?
   Possibilities:
   'The fence posts are concrete and don't look very old.'
   'The bumps and dips in the ground have grass growing on them so they must be quite old.'
   'There is a tree growing on the bank that must have taken years to grow.'
3. With your group examine the site carefully and decide what the purpose of it was. You must show how the evidence supports your theory.
4. What might you hope to find in an excavation to support your theory?

I did the above exercise several times on Cissbury Hill in West Sussex, which boasts a hillfort and hollows in the ground that formed the mouths of Neolithic flint mines. Children from age 7 to 12 came up with various explanations. One was that the site was a launching pad for a flying saucer that landed thousands of years ago (this group could point out barren patches in the ground caused by the immense heat generated by the jets, and a triangle of hollows made by the tripod legs of the saucer). Another suggestion was that the place was a training camp for young warriors (sunken running track around the ditch with vantage points for supervisors etc.). A third idea was that the area was a fortified farm.

The groups presented their explanations in an extremely interesting debate. The point was not whether children could come up with the accepted answers, but rather that they learn to observe and put together evidence to support a reasonable theory. When the accepted explanations of the features were then shown the children examined the evidence critically and with interest.

A third idea is to set up a dig in the school grounds. Problems with this might be (a) that you will need some muscle power to do the initial turf cutting and shifting of topsoil, which will be too much for most children; (b) that you are not likely to find much, if anything. I have heard of teacher's doing this and 'salting' the ground the night before with broken pottery, but this does take away a lot of the point!

Using artefacts to teach about a period

If we really want children to make deductions about what life was like at a particular time in history, they are unlikely to be able to do much by looking at single unrelated items, any more than a visitor could tell a great deal about life in modern Britain by looking at a ball point pen and a pair of trainers. As we saw in the last chapter, our visitor could say something of our level of technology, maybe something about how we attain status, but little about how it feels to live today. If he could look at the entire contents of a child's bedroom, however, then he could say quite a lot about at least a part of modern life.

In the same way we need to look at an *assemblage* of objects to really find out about the past. A good example for Victorian Britain might be laundry equipment. A good set might be:

- a dolly peg (or posser if you live in the North)
- a washboard
- some 'sunlight' soap
- a grater (for the soap)
- a bag of Reckitts Blue (still available)
- old flat irons or slug irons (they open at the back to take a 'slug' of brick heated in the fire) etc.

All these items can be found or bought quite easily.

Things to do

1. Start with a basic analysis of the objects as outlined in the previous chapter. Are the items factory or machine made? This work will tell you something about Victorian society, whether they had factories and good transport to move goods about. Which raw materials were used to make the objects? The most common materials will be wood and iron. Look carefully at the wear on the objects. You will find, for instance, that parts that have been in water often are bleached, parts handled often are dark and stained with sweat, and things heated on an open flame (like goffering irons) are blackened. Can you work out how they were held? What is the most comfortable way to use them?
2. Knowing that the items are laundry equipment, can we work out what they were used for and the sequence in which they were used? Often young children have watched automatic washing machines very carefully, and can see how a dolly, for instance carries out the same task.
3. Having formed your hypothesis about the process, role play it

through. Does it work? Is there an easier/more effective way of doing it?
4. The next stage is to check your hypothesis against available evidence. For a Victorian-style washday there are a number of excellent sources that might be consulted:
   (a) *Oral sources*. There will be plenty of older women in your area who, if not quite Victorian, will readily remember and talk about washdays that used this same equipment. Their evidence is wonderful for details like why you need two flat irons (one to be heating while you use the other). But best of all they can tell you how it felt to be in a kitchen full of steam and heat all day. For further discussion of oral history see Chapter 6.
   (b) *Primary documentary sources*. Mrs Beeton's *Household Management* is good for all things domestic. Many reminiscences of Victorian childhoods like Flora Thompson's *Lark Rise to Candleford* also deal with such matters. If your school is an old one you may find domestic science text books still lying about. Look too at reprinted catalogues for Harrods and other stores, published by David & Charles.
   (c) *Secondary sources*. There are several school books now on the market that talk about Victorian washdays.
5. Ideally the last stage in the exercise will be to use your artefacts and accumulated knowledge in a reconstruction of a Victorian washday at school. You will need woollen and cotton clothing to wash as modern fabrics are far too easy. If you can, get one of your oral history informants to come along and supervise. Many old ladies will take great delight in making sure it gets done properly!

To do all of the above will take a large investment of your time and effort, not to mention valuable teaching hours. Before taking it all on you should be very sure that *you* know what the pay-off is in terms of historical learning. Of course it is a lot more fun than copying from a book, and important lessons about research are being learned, but there should be a major historical point about the period as well.

My justification for this particular project on Victorian laundry would be as follows. It is perfectly tenable that the revolution in domestic technology in the twentieth century has changed women's and thus men's lives more than any other development in the last hundred years. The invention of washing machines, modern fabrics, tumble dryers etc. has saved two days of the 'housewife's' week. It has gone hand in hand with the demise of domestic service as the only prospect for most working-class girls and many boys. It has created the 'leisure market' to deal with all the time saved. No modern child can have any conception of the sheer labour involved in everyday life one hundred years ago without experiencing at least a taste of it. I do not believe that children (or adults) can achieve 'empathy' and enter the souls of people in the past, but I do think that they can be led to a practical understanding that life felt different then. Such understanding leads to questions: Was it all work then? How did people have fun? Was it like this for everyone? The past starts to have logic and reality rather than being just a story.

So, when planning to use assemblages of objects to support the study of a period, look for availability, coherence and a good historical point. For the units on 'Victorian Britain' and 'Britain since 1930' this should not prove too difficult. For the earlier units availability of objects becomes a problem. This can be overcome by using museums and by 'experimental archaeology', which are the subject of the next chapter.

Further reading

—— (1992) *The Teachers Guide to Using Historic Sites.* London: English Heritage.
Good materials on teaching about archaeology can be obtained from:
The Council for British Archaeology
112 Kennington Road, London SE11 6RE
Telephone: 081 582 0494

CHAPTER 4
Using Museums

Picture the scene. One month ago you rang around ten coach companies before you managed to get one for the right day to take your class to the museum. For the last week you have been collecting 'voluntary' parental contributions. Yesterday was the great day: the coach was late, five children were sick almost before you left the car park, and only with great difficulty did you prevent everybody diving into their packed lunches in the first ten minutes. The museum was awash with school groups, some of which were certainly not being disciplined in a way that you felt appropriate. The nagging worries that (a) someone was bound to get lost and (b) Jason was going to start acting up any minute were becoming more and more insistant. In the museum the children separated into three categories: those that had seen it all, Miss, and wanted to go to the shop after ten minutes; those that kept disappearing around corners with very suspicious looks on their faces; and those whom you wished would disappear for two minutes rather than smugly follow you around (preferably holding your hand) saying 'I like museums'. 'It's very interesting'; 'Oh look Miss what's this, isn't Jason being bad! You should have left him behind, Miss'. All this and much much more!

Now on the following day you ask the children to write the traditional 'what we did at the museum' pieces. You collect them in and what do you find?

> Yesterday we went to the Museum. Ravinder was sick on the coach. For lunch I had crips [sic], monster bar and coke. At the shop I bought a dinosaur for my sister, a pen for my mum and an Egyptian Mummy pencil case for me. Jason had a fight with a boy from another school and the Museum man came and told Miss to take him outside.

Of course it is not usually quite as bad as that, but most teachers will recognise some of the above elements from trips they have made. We will not prevent children being children, but school time is far too precious and pressured these days to waste like this. If you are going to a museum as part of a history Study Unit you must try to ensure that genuine historical learning takes place. This requires thought, planning and organisation.

When to go

In the past far too many museum trips were undertaken as the yearly 'class trip'. Usually this took place towards the end of the summer term, and maybe it included a visit to a park or playground to add extra enjoyment to what was seen as a semi-holiday. If one analyses the use of time on such a trip one finds that, say, 50 per cent of it is spent on the coach, 20 per cent spent eating lunch, 5 per cent in the shop, 10 per cent playing, leaving only 15 per cent of time in the museum. It is hardly surprising that the children's writing often reflects this. If you intend to make a museum visit to support historical learning, you must be quite clear exactly what you want the children to gain from the trip, and the timing and object of the visit should follow from that.

I would suggest that there are four common goals for such a trip:

(a) To catch the children's interest and to stimulate their enthusiasm about a particular period.
(b) To allow the children to research with artefacts from a period which are unavailable in the classroom.
(c) To round off a unit, allowing your class of 'experts' to consolidate and enjoy their knowledge of a period, and to look critically at the museum's presentation of it.
(d) To learn about museums as a local amenity, and how to use them.

Obviously if your primary reason is (a), then you need to visit the museum before you start the project. If (b), then the trip should be arranged a couple of weeks into the work. If (c), you should go when most of the classwork has been completed. If the reason is (d), then the timing is less material.

Another factor affecting the timing of visits may be the fact that the material you want the class to see is only temporarily available. Most museums hold thematic exhibitions either of items from their own stores which are rarely on show, or from elsewhere. You should be on the look-out for exhibitions relevant to your needs and grab the opportunities when they occur. The more your children have used museums opportunely, the better they will respond to such occasional out-of-context visits.

Where to go

There are numerous museums in Britain, with very different characteristics, but they mostly fall into four basic types: (1) local museums, (2) national museums, (3) commercially run 'living' or 'working' museums, (4) small specialist museums. Many cross over these boundaries but share certain features. We turn to consider the pros and cons of each type of museum.

(1) Local Museums

Travel time

Obviously if you use your local museum, time wasted in travelling is minimised, and a higher proportion of time can be spent on studying history. Also the trip can be fitted into half a day or even half a morning, which involves no packed lunch, no cancelling swimming, etc. You may even be able to walk there or use public transport, which saves booking coaches.

Cost

Most local museums are run as a public amenity by local library or leisure services. Most still have free entry, at least for school parties. This avoids the necessity of collecting money, and of dealing with parents who cannot afford the cost.

Amenities

Many local museums are short on cloakrooms, toilets etc. But so long as you know this in advance you can make arrangements.

Collection

Every museum has a collection policy. Local museums tend to keep the following: some local archaeological material; material relating to local crafts and industries; social and domestic items often mostly from the last 150 years; material about famous local figures or places. Sometimes they inherit a whole batch of material from a local collector and thus have a speciality like costume or cameras. Most local museums have large collections of photographs, ephemera (posters, playbills, tickets etc.) and paintings of local scenes. They also keep files of historical information about the area. There may well be chronological gaps in their collections: for example, they may have nothing from the Tudor and Stuart period or except perhaps one single spur. Only a proportion of the collection will be on show, with sometimes a great deal in storage.

Educational facilities

Most local museums are very keen to encourage educational visits, not least because their own funding depends on showing the council committee that many local people are using the place. They usually have a small highly qualified but underpaid staff, and many use volunteers as well. It is becoming increasingly common for an education officer to be appointed. The local museum will have much less in the way of pre-prepared educational materials than will larger museums, but will generally be proportionately more willing to arrange the visit your way, provided of course that you convince them that you know what you are doing. Often you can have almost the whole museum to yourself, which means better working conditions for the class, and less administrative and disciplinary headaches for you. At first glance the small museum may look less exciting and more restricted than larger ones, but, provided the material you need to see is there, the interest shown by the children will be entirely dependent on your preparation and organisation.

(2) National museums

Travel time

Almost certainly visiting a national museum will involve hiring a coach and spending quite a long time on it. This is fine if only this museum will serve your purpose; if this is not the case, it is a waste of time.

Cost

Many national museums still have free entry, though some do not. Even if there is no admission charge the cost of travel may still make the trip expensive.

Amenities

National museums will have toilets, cloakrooms, maybe a schools' teaching area and eating area. On the other hand, many are in older buildings with poor access for wheelchairs and they can get very crowded in the summer.

Collection

By their nature national museums are very large and have huge collections. They tend to have most of the really 'exciting' material from particular periods, and things you will find nowhere else. For instance if you are studying Ancient Greece you are unlikely to find anything to look at nearer to your school than the British Museum. In fact the very size of national museums can be a distraction, making it imperative that you are very clear what you are going to look at before you go.

Educational facilities

Virtually all national museums now have education departments, though these range from ten or so full-time staff to a few part-timers. Many have well thought-out and presented educational materials which are usually related to the National Curriculum. The staff work with huge numbers of children in the course of the year and are thus generally very good at their job. The only caveat I would mention is that the materials produced may not be exactly right for your particular children, and it is much harder for national museums to be flexible and talk to you about your specific needs than it is for your local museum to do so. Having said this, most will try very hard to accommodate your requests.

(3) Commercial museums

In this section I am conscious of lumping together a large and diverse group of establishments. For a start many would quarrel with the definition 'commercial', since the museums are usually registered charities. All I really mean is that they are not supported by the government or local authority, and they therefore have to pay much of their upkeep through ticket sales. Because they need the trade of families on 'days out', they must have a large degree of entertainment value. They were often founded by, and are largely run by, enthusiasts who are very committed to, and expert in, subjects like steam engines or tin mining. At best they can be a refreshing change from history in glass cases and really bring the past to life. At worst they amount to a theme park that requires no brain work on the part of the visitor, who simply experiences somebody else's interpretation of the past.

Cost

Entrance fees are high, because such places are expensive to run and need to make a profit (or at least keep losses down).

Amenities

These are generally excellent, with good toilets and plenty of room for eating, teaching, coach parking etc.

Collection

Collections tend to be specialised and include large items like industrial machinery or reconstructed buildings, and you often find things working. Atmosphere is often created by the illusion of really 'being there', with people in costume carrying out period activities in carefully recreated environments. Sometimes children can dress up and join in. All this has great immediacy, children have great fun, and they often learn a lot. The experience is usually a wonderful stimulus to interest about a period, but never forget that recreations are not primary evidence. While children may be very active in their participation, they may be passive in the sense of doing nothing to interpret the artefacts for themselves. There is nothing wrong with this, any more than there is with watching a video or reading a history book. After all we rely on other people's expert presentation of the past for most of our history. But you should be aware at which stages of your study you are asking the children to understand and digest a presentation, and at which you want them to tackle the unprocessed evidence.

Educational facilities

Often highly professional and suitable materials are produced. Staff are usually experienced, though in some of the smaller 'enthusiast-run' places you can end up with someone whom you personally find fascinating but who finds it hard to work at the children's level.

(4) Small specialist museums

I include this category only to signal the fact that there are places that do not fit into any of the above slots but which may be worth a visit. It is difficult to generalise about these museums, but they tend to be small and often well-established. Many owe their origin to a private individual's collection. Some are still run by that individual, while others have been left as a trust.

Cost

Generally there is an entrance fee, but usually it is low.

Amenities

Usually these are very few indeed.

Collection

Small and specialised, e.g. tobacco pipes, motor-cycles, dolls.

Educational facilities

Again, these are usually few or non-existent, but often the Keeper is knowledgeable and co-operative.

Planning your visit

If your class is to study a particular historical period or a theme for a Study Unit, then your first move will be to find out which museums have relevant material. There are a number of museum directories on the market. HMSO print regional guides entitled *Exploring Museums*, and Gene Adams' *Museums and Galleries – a Teachers Handbook* (published by Hutchinson) is also very good. Often museums in a particular area get together to produce their own local guide which you will find in the library or a local museum. Always check with your local museum even if it does not list anything useful: the curators may have something in store which they would be prepared to get out, and they will certainly be able to advise you of the best and nearest places to go. Once you have located possible places *you must make an early preliminary visit yourself*. Go with pencil and paper and work out exactly how your children could usefully spend their time.

First ask at the desk if there are any educational materials already produced for the gallery or area that you are interested in. Museums are getting better and better at making these, but only use them if they really serve the needs of your children. You may decide to produce your own materials and to use a combination of these and the museum's.

Now go and look at the displays and work out the best way for your class to use them. A word of caution: beware of long multi-question worksheets. They can create a scenario familiar to many of us:

> The museum door opens and in rush thirty children clutching worksheets. Question 1 begins 'Look at the model steam engine in the foyer'. Thirty children rush up to the aforementioned engine. In the crush seven of them can actually see it properly. The question goes on to ask 'How many wheels has it got?' The

seven children who can see it count and write down the answer. The others look over their shoulders and copy. Everybody dutifully writes down twelve. Then the whole group moves like a swarm of bees on to the next case . . .

The net result of such a worksheet is that some children glance at a great many objects and find out a lot of fairly trivial details about them which they immediately forget, while most of the class see nothing. The whole process takes a great deal less time than you thought it would, with the result that everybody informs you prematurely that they have finished and they would like to go to the shop.

The purpose of taking the children to the museum is to examine objects, and the activities that you plan must involve really looking at them and thinking about them. To do this the children must (a) be able to see clearly, and (b) spend at least ten or fifteen minutes concentrating on each exhibit or display.

The best way to achieve this is usually to have three or four separate activities around which groups of children rotate. This means that only six or seven children at once will be at any one case or display and they will all be able to see clearly. You may well need extra adult help to supervise the four groups. If so the helpers should be well-briefed and, as far as possible, carefully selected.

The sorts of activities that you should plan include the following:

(1) Observational drawing

Careful drawing requires close observation: it gets the children to really look. You should practise getting the members of your class to make accurate labelled drawings before you go. The children should understand the purpose of the drawing, perhaps to compare the object with a modern equivalent back at school or to form part of a display or book about an aspect of the period that they have selected. Do not give a list of questions followed by an instruction to draw a picture. Instead ask the children to draw first because they will then be much better able to answer any questions. Make sure everyone is properly equipped with a drawing board, pencil and rubber. Tell them how to position themselves, warning them not to lean on the glass, but to sit or stand back from the case.

(2) Oral work

This will probably be your main task on the visit, taking each group in turn. Often the best displays for extended question and answer sessions are tableaux. It is quite common for museums to set up a complete room or workshop scene, a Victorian or Roman kitchen, a blacksmith's shop or a Tudor drawing room (the Museum of London has some good examples). The advantage of these is that they have assemblages of objects in context. As with the analysis of a single object, it is good to start by comparing with the present, and seeing how much can be deduced about the life of the people who used the room from the objects and their position. Take a Victorian kitchen range, for instance:

Q. What is the biggest difference between the range that you see and your cooker at home?
A. *The range works with coal.*
Q. How can you tell that?
A. *You can see the glow and there is a box of coal next to it.*
Q. What processes did people have to go through to use it? . . . and so on.

This kind of structured dialogue leads into a whole deductive recreation of the working day in the kitchen. Children come to realise all the tasks involved, such as collecting dry wood (after a windy night country schools in the last century were often emptied of pupils who were sent wooding by their parents), raking out the ashes (there were no dustmen so people might fill pot holes in the road with the ashes), and going to the coal merchant with a wheelbarrow for some coal. Now get the class to look at all the functions of the range by asking structured questions. You can tell it cooks because there are pans on it; washing is drying over it (relate this to the tumble dryer or use of radiators in the modern home); there are flat irons next to it ready to be heated; clearly it was used to keep people warm since there is an easy chair next to it. Look for clues as to the type of person that lived there – photos on the wall perhaps, or look at the garments that make up the washing. I have never yet encountered a group of children, most of whom did not enjoy this game and did not work out some very sensible answers. Often they will spot things that you have missed.

Obviously you will have to do some research to work out your questions and have some answers of your own. Anecdotes about the past are often the best answers, so collect them avidly. Finally, when in the museum looking at something from the fairly recent past, keep your eyes peeled for the old lady who appears at the back of the group looking scornful or knowing. She is probably longing to come forward and tell you the *real* story about how that iron was used, so *let her*.

(3) Worksheets

Despite my earlier remarks, there is nothing wrong with written questions, provided your children are at the stage when they can use them. It is important, however, that the questions should be such that the child has really to look and think, not just mechanically count or pointlessly distinguish a colour. Open-ended questions that do not have one right answer will ensure that everybody has to think for themselves. Examples might be:

'What do you think x was used for? What is your evidence?'
'How do you think it would feel to wear y? Give five words that would describe the feeling.'

Children who cannot yet read and write easily could work with a parent, who reads the question. The group could then record their answers on a tape machine.

Try to teach concepts and skills through the work that you set. Focus on *how* things have changed, *why* things have changed, what things remain constant, different points of view, time scale and the nature of evidence.

When, before the visit, you have roughed out what you would like to do, talk to the museum staff. Ask for the person in charge of education, tell them your ideas and listen to their advice. Most museum education officers are only too pleased to accommodate teachers who have clear plans, but there may be factors that you are unaware of which would necessitate changes. Apart from anything else, displays change periodically, and it would be a pity to plan everything around something that has disappeared when the children arrive. The officer will probably have other suggestions as well, which may be even better than yours (or mine).

Special arrangements

Usually it is much easier to get special facilities in a small museum, but even these are now much busier with school parties and you should not take them for granted. Museums have an obligation to make anything in their care available for scholarly research, but this is counterbalanced by another obligation to conserve their collection and, as far as possible, keep it from any deterioration at all. If you can show that your children are serious researchers, who need to look at evidence, then many museums will get things out of store especially for your class to look at. The curators, however, will be very nervous about large numbers of children being near valuable items, and they will only do it if they have a suitable space and you can convince them that you and your class know what they are doing. Whatever you do, avoid telling curators what to do, and be ostentatious about fulfilling any conditions they impose. Once they trust you they can be very cooperative. Many museums have schools handling collections, mystery objects etc. which can easily be layed on, so making your visit more enjoyable and useful.

Loan collections

There are a number of museum loan collections around the country. Some are county-wide, some very small and based on one museum. If there is such a scheme near you, find out the details. Most schemes will not lend outside their own area. Museums are extremely unlikely to loan anything except those items specially earmarked for such a collection. These will usually have been chosen because they are relatively common, unprovenenced (i.e. no one knows exactly where they came from, so they are less important archaeologically), and generally expendable. This means that you might be able to borrow some decent stone axes or pieces of Roman pottery and any amount of Victorian stuff, but Saxon, Viking or Tudor material is liable to be thin on the ground.

Heading all the above advice may seem to involve you in a great deal of work, but it is a recipe for a successful visit that can form the basis of much useful study for your class, both before and after the visit. During my own time as a museum education officer I occasionally met teachers who fought shy of any planning, saying that they wanted the children to be free to look around for themselves. Whilst I am all in favour of 'browsing' in museums, I do not think that it works as a school visit. I noticed that often children who had made a structured visit to the museum, with their school, would return with their parents or alone, on a Saturday or in the holidays. Also the 'slicker' your planning the less you will have to worry about bad behaviour. Try to know in advance every move from putting away coats to counting the children back on to the coach. Make sure the class know exactly what they are going to find out and what they will have to do before they go. If there are no toilets at your chosen destination check around the area. As well as public ones, local schools, churches or community centres will often let you use theirs if you make arrangements in advance. Lastly, and nothing to do with history, keep counting the class, don't let the children eat on the coach, and keep the windows open even in winter. The children may freeze, but at least they won't be sick.

Further reading

The Group for Education in Museums (GEM) organises seminars, and local and national meetings. They also publish *The Journal of Education in Museums*, which is useful. Their address is :
> The Group for Education in Museums
> Jeni Harrison (Membership Secretary)
> The Old Manse of Lynturk
> Muir of Fowlis
> Alford
> Aberdeen AB33 8HS

Exploring Museums London (HMSO) – individual volumes available for the different regions.

Adams, G. (1989) *Museums and Galleries – a Teachers Handbook*. London: Hutchinson.

CHAPTER 5
Experimental Archaeology

The title of this chapter may seem rather removed from the classroom, but primary school history teachers have been carrying out experimental archaeology for a long time, if not always under that title, and it is an exciting and very useful technique. In essence, experimental archaeology involves trying out a hypothesis about life in the past by recreating, as far as possible, past conditions and then carrying out experiments. The classic example, in this country, was Butser Hill Experimental Farm in Hampshire.

Quite a number of farm sites from the Celtic Iron Age of southern England have been excavated this century. They yield a lot of useful evidence. There are always plenty of post holes set out in various patterns: large circles, small triangles, etc. There are often deep pits in the ground. There are fireplaces. Scattered about there are broken pottery, rusted ironwork and the occasional bigger artefact. Burnt grains tell us which crops were grown, while animal bones tell us which beasts were kept or hunted. This evidence leaves a number of questions unanswered. What were the pits for? What structures left the post holes?

Archaeologists come up with different explanations. One expert says that the pits were for rubbish, the evidence being that some of them contain broken pottery and animal bones. But another expert points out that the pits do not all contain these things. Many seem to be lined with clay, and anyway digging them would take a lot more effort than is usually expended on refuse disposal. Perhaps they were for storing something, maybe grain: after all, arable farmers have to store grain somewhere. The first group then come back and indicate the small triangles of post holes. Clearly they are tripodal supports for raised grain stores. These would keep the grain from rats and damp.

We cannot return to the Iron Age and find out which explanation is correct (maybe both are or neither). What we can do is try out the hypotheses to determine if they are viable. In other words we can build a pit store, line it with clay, fill it with the same kind of grain as the

Iron Age farmers used, seal it and leave it for a year. If the grain all rots, or the rats get it, then either the pits were not grain stores or you have done something wrong in the way that you built or used it.

At Butser, Peter Reynolds conceived and brought into operation a much more ambitious plan. A farm is a coherent entity: all the processes that go on in it must harmonise and fit in with one another. Butser pooled all the available evidence about Celtic farming on the Downs, and attempted to recreate a working farm for a long-term experiment. Considerable trouble was taken to get everything right. Pigs with bones that matched those of Iron Age swine were obtained by crossing European wild boar with Tamworth sows. Soay sheep and Dexter cattle were selected. Spelt and Emmer wheat was grown. The buildings followed the post hole plan of genuine sites and the experimenters worked out the most practical and effective superstructures using available technology.

The reconstructed farm has run for a number of years and it has produced a great deal of interesting data on the possibilities and problems of farming in the Iron Age. Until recently a second site was open to the public, and this was an excellent place for a school visit. Unfortunately this is now closed, but, at the time of writing efforts are being made to find a new location.

Experimental archaeology can be undertaken at many levels. You cannot rebuild an Iron Age farm on the school site but there are a great many things that you can do. If your children make hypotheses about how Victorian laundry implements were used, you could encourage them to try to wash clothes using that method. They are then carrying out experimental archaeology. In this particular example you will have other sources, written and oral, against which to check your findings. When dealing with an earlier period of history, however, you can find genuine mysteries to solve. These need not take a lot of resources. The following example was the result of site and museum visits.

Digging in the New Stone Age

Some ten-year-olds and I had been looking at the remains of Neolithic Flint Mines on the Downs above Worthing, and we had talked a great deal about Stone Age technology. In the local museum the children saw the shoulder blades of cattle, which, the label said, were found on the site and had been used as shovels. Similar bone 'shovels' have been found near Neolithic and Bronze Age earthworks. Someone remarked that it did not look like a very good shovel to her, and I had to agree that it did not seem a particularly effective tool. This might have passed as an example of 'the primitive stupidity of Stone Age people' if we had not been stressing throughout the project that within the limits of resources available, people then were as skilful and expert as we are today. We decided to try out bone shovels and see if they worked. Perhaps the archaeologists had got it wrong and the 'shovels' were in fact something completely different.

First of all we visited the local butcher (not a pleasant experience for a vegetarian like myself), and found out which day he did his jointing. He promised to save us two cow shoulder blades. The next stage was particularly distressing for me as it involved filling my usually meat-free kitchen with the smell of boiling flesh as I removed all traces from the bones. It is very important to have bones completely clean, bleached and disinfected before children handle them.

Next we compared our bones with those in the museum. It was immediately apparent that modern cows are much bigger than their ancestors. This thought led us into the subject of selective breeding and developments in agriculture. But generally it was agreed that we could use our shovels in a fair test.

To make our test useful we had first to establish what materials were to be shovelled. A visit to a disused chalk pit yielded a pile of chalk rubble such as one might have to shift when mining into the Downs.

Initially we just tried out the bones on the chalk, using them like a coal shovel. We found them very clumsy. In fact one could not really move any chalk without using one's hand to keep it on the bone. Some children still thought it was easier than using their hands alone, so we did a time and motion study. In a series of timed tests, 'hand users' consistently outperformed 'shovel and hand users' in moving the same pile of chalk the same distance.

The children concluded that the bones could not have been shovels. But this left the problem of their presence on so many sites where digging had taken place. I found another answer in a paper about some earthworks in Wessex. The archaeologist there had asked the same questions as us and had carried out the same sort of tests. But he had gone one stage further and tried different ways of using the bone. He and his colleagues found that if you held it like a dagger and scraped backwards into a basket held between your shins, then the cow's shoulder blade worked very well indeed. Unfortunately, by the time I discovered this, our school project was over so I could not recreate his experiment with the children.

Stone Age technology

The Stone Age is a wonderful period for experimental archaeology, partly because there are a lot of real questions to be answered and partly because the technology involved is comparatively simple. Unfortunately the National Curriculum for history does not include a unit which covers 'prehistory' as such. The Unit on food and farming, however, does explicitly start with Neolithic farming, and therefore provides an opportunity to study this very long and important period of our past. The local history Units could also be used, especially in areas which provide plenty of evidence of prehistoric activity. The Key Stage 1 Unit can certainly accommodate Stone Age studies. (Incidentally, please do not entitle such studies 'Cavemen', since for most of the period, in most of the country, people did not live in caves, and the term gives them a subhuman sound.) Time spent on looking at the Stone Age will be well spent since it can also involve some relevant aspects of geography because the relationship between humans and their local environment was very close in the Stone Age. Additionally, some work on science and technology is needed to test local resources and their properties.

Working with flint

If you have looked at stone tools in the class or the museum then you can learn a great deal more by trying to make some. I should say initially that though many experimental archaeology projects are quite possible with Key Stage 1 children, flint working is not. You need some strength to knap (work) flint and it is very sharp. I have done such work successfully with children from about nine years of age upwards.

First you need some flint. Flint comes in two forms: pebbles, which you can find on a beach, and cores. Cores are large, irregularly shaped lumps which usually occur in chalk Downland. The pebbles have been abraded by the sea and other pebbles into smaller, rounder stones. Cores are much better than pebbles to work with, but in practice you will probably end up using pebbles as they are much easier to find. You can sometimes find good cores in disused chalk pits (they are marked on Ordnance Survey maps), but do not trespass or take anything without permission. You can also find cores on some beaches where the sea is acting directly on to a chalk cliff. Find the largest and bulkiest pieces you can; those with long thin projections are not much use. If you have to use pebbles, then look for the biggest. You will also need hammer stones, nice spherical flints as heavy as your knappers can comfortably handle.

Next you need safety equipment: flint knapping can be dangerous. Strong eye protectors, which should be amongst your science gear, will protect against flying chips. They should be worn by *everyone* in the area in which flint knapping is taking place. The school science resources also often include plastic aprons, and it is well if your flint knappers wear these too. Lastly gardening gloves are needed if cut hands are to be avoided. Wherever possible do your knapping outside and away from windows that might break. It is better to work on concrete than grass as it will be easier to clear up all the small sharp debris afterwards.

The simplest form of knapping is done using the hammer stone. It is spherical because that makes it less likely to break than the piece you are working on as you hit the two together. First you must learn to break the flint. Hold the hammer stone like a ball in your writing hand. Take another piece of flint in the other hand and hold it out in front of you with the bit you want to knock off, projecting as far away from your fingers as possible. Strike down with the hammer stone, giving a flick of the wrist as you strike. Flint is brittle and it should break clean and sharp, though it takes a little practice. Because the stone is heavy, children often want to lay the flint on the ground and pound it. This will not work. Only with practice will you learn to predict which way the stone is likely to break, though generally of course it will crack at the thinnest and weakest point. Experiment by changing the angle at which you strike to make it break the way you want it to.

The beautifully crafted Neolithic axes which you can see in a museum or in books were made from flint which was mined from deep in the ground. This has fewer flaws than stone from shallower depths, and cracks in nice straight lines. Those axes were also made by masters of the art, and it is worth knapping just to appreciate their skill. You and your children cannot expect to create such pieces, but you can make usable tools. Basically these tools will be of two sorts, core tools and flake tools. In the case of a core tool you knock off pieces from a pebble till it is the shape that you require. Flake tools are made from the small pieces struck off a larger one.

For children, flake tools are easiest. If you take a long thin pebble you should be able to knock off a number of small flakes from it like slices. You want to produce pieces with as little of the outer crust of the flint on them as possible. Many will come off with *very* sharp edges, so handle with care. Straight away you can demonstrate what

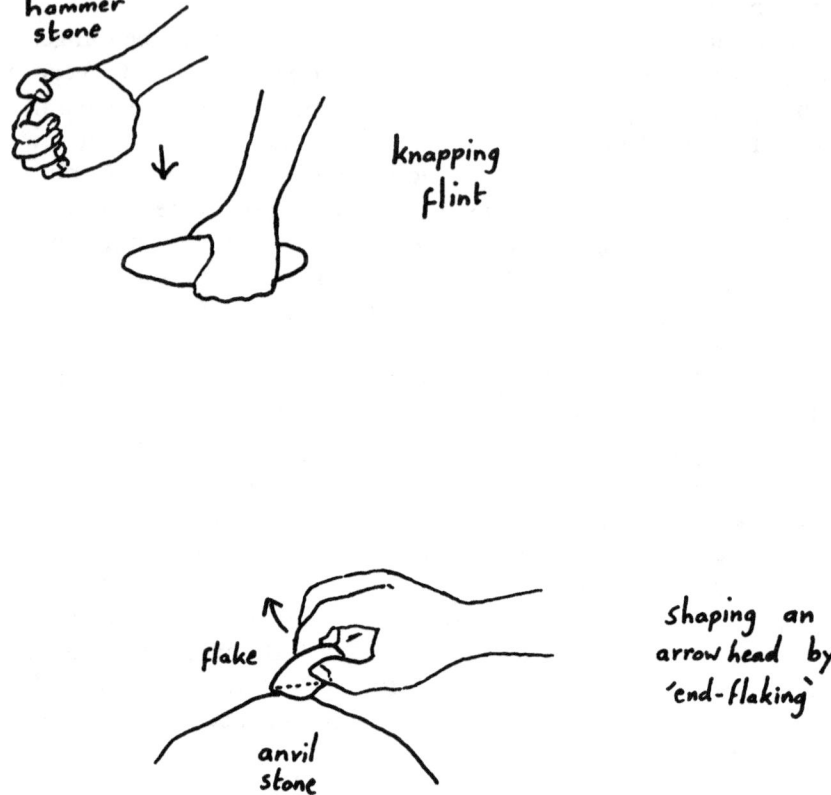

Figure 5.1 Flint knapping techniques

an effective cutting material flint is by trying it on paper, leather etc. It will go through leather like a Stanley knife. Many flakes will already look like tools, arrow heads, knives or scrapers. There are several techniques for finishing them.

For 'end-flaking', you need a nice big flat 'anvil' of flint placed on the ground. Look for a chip that is thin and fairly even in thickness and decide how you want to shape it. A 'leaf shaped' arrow head is a good thing to try. It can be shaped by grasping the flake between finger and thumb and breaking off unwanted material by pressing down sideways on to the anvil stone.

As you work you will produce a large number of very small sharp pieces which can be used to make 'composite tools', that is, tools made of different materials. To make a sickle you need a curved branch of fairly strong dead wood. Cut it off at about half a metre long (ideally of course you would do this by chopping a V-shaped notch with a sharpened flint and then breaking it). The thickest end will be the handle of the sickle, so leave room to grasp it. Then make a long slot along the inner length of the curve, using a small pointed flint. Your little sharp flakes can then be stuck into the groove to make a jagged saw edge. In the Stone Age glue made from wood resin was probably used, so a modern resin glue is not too out of character. The small flints used in this way are known as 'microliths'.

If you get interested in flint knapping there are more refined techniques to try, but you will probably need to locate an expert to help you. There are a surprising number of enthusiasts and serious researchers in the field. Grimes Graves in Norfolk is a Neolithic Flint Mine which children can visit and actually descend. They also know a lot about flint knapping there. University College London's Institute of Archaeology would know of people interested, and even local archaeological societies often include flint enthusiasts among their members. The *Shire Album* on later Neolithic stone tools has some information on the subject.

Pottery

If you and/or your class are keen on pottery then you will find it very useful to spend time looking into, and trying out, early techniques. Potters will be able to work out detail better than I, but here are some ideas that I have tried with success:

Digging clay

Children who have always used pre-prepared clay from a bag will get a better idea of how people in the past used their environment if they have the experience of digging, cleaning and using local clay. If you live in an area like the Thames Basin then your school may well be sitting on a bed of excellent clay, underneath the topsoil. There may be some exposed on a local building site, which you could get permission to dig. I have cleaned clay by breaking it up and mixing it with water to a near-liquid form to strain off the biggest stones, then leaving it in buckets to settle, and pouring off the excess water. Putting lumps on a wooden board will dry it still further till it is workable. You will find examples of the early pottery made in your area in the local museum. With luck your children will be able to see that it was made from the same sort of clay as they have prepared. Bronze Age urns are not too difficult to copy using a 'coil pot' technique.

Bush firing

I have taken this subtitle from Harvey's *Imaginative Pottery* (A & C Black) which is the source of most of my technical knowledge about pottery. In this manual you will find full details of how to fire pottery without a kiln. You should be warned that it is a major operation which is impractical unless you have substantial grounds away from neighbours, and a lot of commitment. However, it is a great project to try. Kilns were not introduced to Britain until the late Iron Age. The 'inclusions' in pottery fabric mentioned earlier were there to strengthen the pot in bush firing and you could carry out some interesting experiments on the merits of different sorts of inclusion.

Samian ware

On one occasion a class of children and I made an experiment into how this type of moulded pottery was made in Roman times. We have good evidence of how the makers of Samian Ware went about it because several moulds of the standard designs used on this attractive mass-produced Roman pottery have been found. You need to use the finest red clay that you can find if you want the finished product to look at all like the real thing. The mould for, say a bowl, would be thrown on a wheel. I cannot throw pottery so I used a bowl from my kitchen to mould the mould. I carefully lined the inside of a small bowl with clay to about one centimetre thick and cut any excess away at the top. I had oiled the bowl first so that the clay mould would be easy to get out. I then scraped and burnished the inside of the clay mould to get it perfectly smooth. Once your mould is made you can decorate the inside with incised designs, which will give you a pattern in low relief on the finished bowls as you use the mould. The mould must be fired in the kiln and it can then be used to mass produce bowls. Again a Shire Publication, Swan's *Pottery in Roman Britain* is a good source for pictures of real Samian designs.

Votive offerings

Excavations in Roman temple sites often yield interesting little clay models, sometimes of a leg or an arm, perhaps of an animal. These 'votive offerings' were used to bring the gods' attention to, say, a sprained ankle, in the case of the leg model, in the hope that the said god would cure it. Or they might be thank-you gifts to the god for a cure or a birth or some other benefit. This practice is continued in

Sicily and other parts of the world even today, though the offerings in Sicily are of course now to saints rather than gods. If children have seen these models they might like to make some, though it is stretching a point to call this experimental archaeology since there is no real experiment involved.

It is difficult to do much pottery work for later periods of history at primary level since most pottery was thrown on a wheel.

Spinning, weaving and dying

Spindle whorls and loom weights are common archaeological finds from periods down to medieval times. The former are usually in the form of roughly disc-shaped stones with a hole in the middle. The shaft of the spindle was a stick about thirty centimetres long, which was pushed through the hole to protrude by a small amount. A hank of carded wool was wrapped around another stick, the distaff, which rested on the shoulder or in the crook of the arm. Wool was pulled from the distaff and twisted on to the spindle, the spinning of which, whilst continuously feeding out wool, created thread. The process is quite within the capabilities of junior children, who often find it a great deal of fun, in probable contrast to their ancestresses who were often expected to be spinning whenever their hands were not otherwise occupied. Again the process is easier to demonstrate than describe, and experts perhaps from a local society of spinners and weavers should be called in. There are many such societies and they are usually very willing to help. Libraries and tourist information offices carry lists of local societies. Raw wool can be bought through craft suppliers, or if you live near sheep fields it can be harvested from the barbed wire.

Loom weights look very much like doughnuts made of stone or clay. The warp threads hung down vertically from a simple frame loom and were weighted at the bottom. The weft thread was then woven in and out of them and pushed up tight with a comb. Making such a loom is not particularly difficult but it is less useful in the classroom than spinning, in my experience, since only one person can use it at a time wheras you can easily make thirty spindles, and disentangling messes can become a full-time occupation.

Dying spun thread or woven cloth with the natural dies available locally would again have been a normal practice through most of history. Take advice from experts, but oak and privet leaves, onion skins, blackberries and carrots are all common and will produce interesting colours when boiled with your wool.

Food

Children generally enjoy cooking, and using historic processes and recipes is a well-tried activity. It is only really experimental when you work from an artefact like a saddle quern or a mortarium and find the best way to use it. However, just following recipes can literally give the flavour of the period and is well worth doing. For recipes relating to particular periods, English Heritage's series *Food and Cooking in Roman (Prehistoric, Medieval, 16th Century, 17th Century, 19th Century) Britain* is very good, and easily obtainable.

Structures

The most fun that I and my pupils have had in the field of experimental archaeology has undoubtedly been whilst building huts. It has also proved to be an activity with huge educational payoff in historical, geographical, technological and scientific learning. To do it properly you need room and some effort goes into finding materials, but the work itself is not too difficult.

What sort of a structure you decide to build would, of course, depend on the period being studied, but basic wattle and daub construction was used in many parts of the country from the New Stone Age down to at least the seventeenth century. Even if you cannot build a hut you can experiment with a short run of walling or roof, which will give insight into the methods used to construct historic buildings in your area.

Wattle and daub

Wattle is made by weaving flexible rods or laths in and out of vertical rigid poles, called sails. The process is still used to make sheep hurdles, and demonstrations of hurdle making are not uncommon at county shows and similar events today. From the Stone Age to early medieval times, the usual vernacular practice was to push posts of three or four centimetres in diameter into the ground about thirty centimetres apart, and to weave thinner rods of hazel or willow in and out. The sort of wood is important because different species have different properties. Hazel is flexible and strong and has been grown in coppices for thousands of years to provide long thin shoots. Ash is more rigid and straight and makes good 'sails'. During the Middle Ages it became usual to make a massive box-frame for a house in oak, but the spaces were still filled with wattle and daub. The daub with which the wattle is plastered is a mixture of clay, soil, cow manure, chopped straw and chalk or lime. The precise quantities of each would vary, and make a

Figure 5.2 A hut built by Year 4 children in West Sussex

fit subject for experiment. We always found it most effective and satisfying to apply the daub with our hands.

We thatched our Stone and Iron Age huts, with advice and old reed thatch obtained from a local thatcher. The children may not have done a professional job, but our huts stood up to gales that removed a good part of the school roof!

There is not space here to go into full details of building huts, and if you decide to try it, or many of the other ideas that I have touched on, then you will almost certainly need to find help from local craftsmen, foresters, archaeologists, curators and enthusiasts. It will take a great deal of commitment and preparation, but it is worth it and you will find that there is plenty of help and expertise available if you practice the basic teacher's skill of having the cheek to ask for everything, free, in the sacred name of education!

Further reading

Harvey, D. (1983) *Imaginative Pottery*. London: A & C Black.
Swan, V. (1988) *Pottery in Roman Britain*. Princes Risborough: Shire.
Pitts, M. (1980) *Later Stone Implements*. Princes Risborough: Shire.

Renfrew, J. (1985) *Food and Cooking in Prehistoric Britain*. London: English Heritage.

Renfrew, J. (1985) *Food and Cooking in Roman Britain*. London: English Heritage.

Black, M. (1985) *Food and Cooking in Medieval Britain*. London: English Heritage.

Brears, P. (1985) *Food and Cooking in 16th Century Britain*. London: English Heritage.

Brears, P. (1985) *Food and Cooking in 17th Century Britain*. London: English Heritage.

Black, M. (1985) *Food and Cooking in 19th Century Britain*. London: English Heritage.

Reynolds, P. (1979) *Iron Age Farm*. London: British Museum.

CHAPTER 6
Oral History

As we turn from artefacts to the use of oral history, we move, in many ways, to the opposite pole of the sphere of evidence. While objects are concrete in themselves and to that extent yield objective information, direct oral accounts are subjective in their nature, even before we start to interpret them. With objects we are often frustrated with the fact that they cannot talk and we cannot ask questions, but with an oral informant we can do just that. Evidence from artefacts is often general and practical, whereas oral testimony is sometimes very personal. Many of the best results of artefact work with children come because of the questions which the pupils formulate while studying the objects, and this stimulates and directs research. Much of the best oral history work, on the other hand, is done after research, by informed questioners. Its greatest contribution can be that by supplying the feelings that go with the facts, it adds the detail that turns a historical account into real life. Especially with the youngest children, it is this reality that matters. They believe the story best from someone who can say 'I was there'.

In Chapter 1 I made a distinction between directly communicated memories and the 'oral tradition'. This distinction bears repetition. The oral tradition is the way in which history is passed down without the use of writing. It is undoubtedly the oldest form of history. In some cultures, particularly illiterate ones, the process is very formal. We know from the Irish epics that the three orders of Druids spent long years in apprenticeship, much of the time devoted to the learning by heart of geneologies, stories of past events, songs, laws and legal precedents. The person of a druid was sacrosanct and demanded great respect because he (or she, there are, I believe, some accounts of female druids) carried in his head information necessary to preserve the fabric of society. In any dispute, or in time of disaster or war, the ruler consulted the druid to find out the correct course of action, the correct course being the traditional one, or at least one that could be justified in terms of tradition.

Because of the weight attached to this 'formal' sort of oral tradition within the cultures that use or once used it, it is capable of passing very large bodies of information word-perfect over very long periods of time. It is due to this phenomenon that we have any accounts at all of pre-literate times. The Old Testament of the Christian Bible and Homer's *Iliad* as well as the Irish *Book of Conquests* were passed down in this manner for many generations before they were written down.

This formal oral tradition is different in many respects from direct oral testimony. It lacks the immediacy and reality of the latter and its study may seem to belong rather to the section on documentary evidence. This book, however, is about the nature of evidence. It is about teaching children to look at evidence in as 'scientific' a way as possible (without detracting in any way from the romance and pleasure of the subject). 'Scientifically' the oral tradition and direct oral testimony must be approached in the same way, because both are 'retrospective'. When you speak to relatives about life in the war you are not necessarily hearing exactly what they thought then because their experience has been filtered through their subsequent life to leave only what they need of it, or what was so powerful that they cannot forget. In the same sort of way events in Bronze Age Greece were filtered to leave the epic of the *Iliad*.

Which sort of oral evidence you use will depend quite simply upon which period you are studying. With no trouble you can find informants who will talk about 'Britain since 1930'. You may find a genuine Victorian (though not for much longer). You can get accounts of things that had not changed since late Victorian times quite easily. There are epics to look at for 'Invaders and Settlers' and 'Ancient Greece'. There is folklore, song and story for 'Tudors and Stuarts', 'Ships and Seafarers' and many local studies. Most of this chapter, however, will be devoted to finding and using direct oral testimony

Finding informants

The sort of informant that you seek will depend on two main factors: what you want to know and how you want to use the person. How you use the person may in turn depend on their 'presence', availability and ability to talk to children. Especially with infants, the physical presence of an older person talking about the past in an informal way is a very natural and effective method of learning history. At Key Stage 1 the syllabus is much more open to use of any good informant. Finding a speaker on 'schooldays in grandmother's time' for instance, is not difficult, and gives you scope to choose carefully whom you use.

As a teacher you will know the sort of speaker who can hold the attention of your class, but unfortunately it is not easy to gauge how someone unused to talking to a class of children will react to being put in that situation. It is often best to choose someone who you know well enough to 'control'. There is nothing worse than the embarassment of watching your class become bored, disinterested and badly behaved because the speaker has 'lost them'. You end up trying to give your errant pupils inconspicuous 'black looks' whilst attempting to stop your honoured guest without giving offence. Using your own relatives is often a very good idea. The children love meeting your mum, and you can brief her in advance and shut her up when you want to. Retired teachers are thick on the ground and good material. Having said these things, there are, of course, plenty of other wonderful informants about.

In some cases you will want to find people with much more specific memories to share. Maybe you want old pupils of the school, or people who worked down a local pit, or memories of the 'home front' in your area during the last war. There are two excellent and well-tried methods of finding such speakers. The first is the local newspaper(s). These are often read regularly by the older members of the community. The editor will usually be only too pleased to run an article to the effect that 'Grove School seeks past pupils', with the aid of a photo of your children brandishing slates and the old school bell. If not, a letter would certainly be printed. Usually the response is very good, though it will be less in areas that have a more shifting population. A second avenue to explore is the local old people's homes, day centres and sheltered housing. Ring up the warden first and allow them to make enquiries: they often know who would be good and willing. As with so many other points, ask the local museum, they may well know of informants. They may also know of local oral history recordings that may be available.

One last suggestion relates to topics on 'evacuation' during the Second World War, justly a favourite in primary schools. You will find in your research that children from your school were evacuated to one particular town, or that children from another town were evacuated to yours. This information will be in the school log book for the relevant years. Write to the local paper in that other town to find evacuees or families who took them in. You can find the address of the local paper by ringing up the Town Hall Tourist Information Department, or by consulting the relevant volume of *Yellow Pages*.

Using informants

The first stage in using informants effectively is to decide what you want to get from them. The golden rule to observe when thinking about this is to remember that you are dealing with people this time, not objects. People's memories, with very few exceptions, do not work in perfect linear progression, with dates in the margin and names in bold type. When we remember names and dates many of us remember them wrongly. We place things in time by our own personal landmarks – 'I remember Sue was still in a pushchair when we went there, so it must have been about 1960.' People remembering events of fifty years ago often get things in the wrong order, and if they are remembering their childhood then they might have had a completely erroneous impression of what was going on even at the time. If you are interviewing a public figure such as an ex-cabinet minister or a trade union official then he or she may be able to give a coherent account of national events, probably with the aid of diaries in which to check facts. Most of us are concerned for most of the time only with getting the job in hand done and what we will have for supper. We only really remember wider events when they impinged on our world. I lived as a child through the 'Suez Crisis', but all I know about it was learned much later. What I do recall vividly is the soldiers who patronised my father's cafe giving me badges before they 'went to Suez'. Whether they actually did go there I could not say.

The best use of oral history informants, then, is not on the whole to get a lot of hard facts, but rather to get impressions, feelings and details. Best of all they can tell stories. An amusing anecdote about when Mrs Williams was a naughty girl at school is worth pages of facts from books about school life in the past.

The trouble sometimes is that the informant does not always understand that this is what you want. They often, quite rightly, attach great importance to helping in children's education so they try to sound as much like a history book as possible. Another common response is to clam up and give very short or one word answers to the children's carefully prepared questions: Q. 'Did you have a school uniform?', A. 'No'. To get the best evidence you must ask the right questions in the right environment, with the right stimulus. (I have used stimulants in the form of beer in the past, but not in school!)

The right questions are those that cannot be answered in one word. They should lead the person to picture the past and describe it. 'Can you remember what you used to wear to school?' is better than 'Did you have a school uniform?' People often remember key occasions much better than generalities. 'Can you remember what you wore on your first day at school?' may well set the memory off nicely. I have found that 'Can you remember what you were doing when you heard war was declared?' was an almost foolproof method of warming up wartime informants. The interviewee will often lead off into generalities of their own accord after you have prompted to recall particular events or circumstances. After Mr Jones has described the feeling of those awful scratchy trousers to his satisfaction and yours, he will happily talk about the pinafore dresses that the girls wore.

Other 'right questions' will relate to what the informant has already told you. I once accompanied some teenage girls who were interviewing a lady about the war years. She had just given a lengthy answer to a question, in the course of which she spoke of her daughter who was a nurse. The girl who was interviewing, who clearly was not really listening, woke up with a start as she finished speaking, referred to her list and asked her next prepared question: 'Have you got any children?' The old lady looked with disgust at this stupid girl who was wasting her time, and took little interest in helping any further. If in contrast you ask supplementary questions about what has just been said, the informant is reassured that you are interested and paying attention, and will be encouraged to tell you more.

Informants can be helped in their journey back in time by period stimuli. Photographs are very good for this. An old school photo, for instance, may well get an old pupil started without any question at all. 'That's Mr Brown standing at the side . . . He was a strict one. If there was a fight in the playground he'd come out with his cane . . .'. As I have already implied, oral history work often fits best into a project after some initial research has already been done. This means that you can show the informant your 'work in progress' and invite their comments. If you have gathered some artefacts from the period, for example ration books, then let the informant see and handle them. They will help to prompt memories.

Sometimes using stimuli can have surprising results. I once visited a lady who had answered a newspaper appeal for wartime evacuees to Worthing. I took with me an album of press cuttings that had been compiled by another informant, and started the interview by showing it. The lady, 'Alice', had turned over only a couple of pages when she stopped, obviously deeply moved by what she saw. She had found herself confronted by a photo of herself aged four, arriving at Worthing station, clutching her sister's hand. The occasion had formed a major break in her life as she had never really lived with her mother again. The interview carried on with great feeling and some tears. I learned a great deal that day. Although I was already familiar with the details of evacuation from documentary sources, I now *felt* something about it.

This brings us to the 'right place' for interviews. There is often a conflict here. The best place for you is in school, but the best place for interviewees is often one where they feel at home. I do not think that 'Alice' would have opened up, as she did, in a classroom full of children. There are several alternative methods of carrying out the interviews:

1. The interviewee comes to your classroom and talks to the whole class. At Key Stage 1 this is probably the best tactic. Your informant will probably not be too intimidated by a lot of small children sitting around her on the carpet. The conversation will probably be three-way, with you and the children joining in.
2. Small groups of children visit the informant and tape interviews. This method needs much more organisation. Obviously the groups must be accompanied, and you will need a lot of informants and adult help if the whole class is to participate. You cannot be in several places at once, so your adult helpers will need training in interview technique. It will be much easier to organise with the help of an Old People's Home or Day Centre, where at least it can all take place under one roof.
3. The interviewee comes to school and is interviewed on tape by a small group. This method is often the easiest and best. Some informants will need transport.
4. The teacher visits the interviewees alone in their own homes and uses the tapes in school. This method will often produce the best interviews, though some older people respond better to children than adults. You will have to commit a great deal of your own time, so you will only do it if you are personally interested. The big disadvantage is that 'immediacy' is lost if the children do not meet the informant and ask the questions themselves.

Interview technique and using tape recorders

Before interviewing, the interviewers should have devoted some time and thought to the questions they intend to ask (see my comments above on 'right questions'). They should have prepared an outline of these, but it is important that they realise that it is just an outline not a script. Try to cover the topics you have prepared, but try to allow the conversation to follow freely and try to let the informant say what she wants to.

You should keep a written record with the tape. This may be a typed form which notes the name and address of the interviewee, the time and date of the interview, the names of the interviewers, the topics covered in the tape, also any photos or other material referred to in it.

Test your tape recorder and tape before leaving the classroom. If it is battery-operated, have a spare set to hand. Do not forget that the mains sockets in old houses may not match your 13 amp plug. Make sure that you have plenty of blank tape. Just before interviewing, test the recorder again asking the interviewee to tell you something unimportant, like what they had for breakfast, to check the relative volumes of your voices and thus where to place the microphone. If you use a hand-held microphone then wrap the lead once around your hand: this prevents clicking noises from loose connections. It is often less distracting for the interviewee if one child concentrates on operating the recorder and holding the mike, and another child does the talking.

Do not forget, and never let your children forget, that your informants are giving you a gift of their memories. They deserve to be treated with respect and courtesy, but also with friendship before, during and after the interview. Do not just drop them once you have what you want. They may well appreciate seeing the results of your work, and letters of thanks from the children are of course essential.

Interviewers must develop 'The BBC nod'. Normal conversation is full of interjections – 'Mm, yes . . . really . . . how wonderful'. These sound very stupid on tape. But if you make no response to what the informant is saying they tend to dry up. The answer is to nod and smile at strategic points in the conversation, reassuring the informant that you are interested without making distracting noises. You will feel silly doing this at first, and the class can have great fun practising on one another.

At the end of the interview the informant may well want to hear some of it back. If they do not mind, it is also nice to have a photograph of each informant.

When you return to base, make very sure that the tapes are properly labelled and put away with their attached record sheet before anyone rushes off to play.

What to do with your collected material

To use the material on the tapes effectively, all or part of it will probably have to be transcribed at some point. Even in the case of a class talk at Reception level you will need to be able to remind the children of exactly what was said. If you do not do this then you are not giving the text the respect due to primary evidence. As in all planning you should start with the concepts and skills that you are working on. For instance the National Curriculum Statements of Attainment at Levels 1 and 2 suggest that pupils should be able to:

> Place in sequence events in a story about the past. (AT1 L1).
> Suggest reasons why people in the past acted as they did. (AT1 L2).
> Identify differences between past and present times. (AT1 L2).
> Show an awareness that different stories about the past can give different versions of what happened. (AT2 L2).
> Communicate information acquired from an historical source. (AT3 L1).
> Recognise that historical sources can stimulate and help answer questions about the past. (AT2 L2).
>
> DES (1991) *History in the National Curriculum*

A sequencing activity might involve individuals drawing pictures to illustrate events in a story told by your informant. They might be encouraged to use artefacts or photos to add one piece of period detail to their pictures. Sequence them together as a class while listening to the tape. Ask the children to put up their hands as they hear the key words that go with the next picture. Write up these key quotations and put them up on the wall beside the sequenced pictures.

Act out the story, discussing what the different characters were thinking and why they acted as they did. Get the children to pick out differences between then and now while listening to the tape. Make a 'then and now' display that contrasts modern things to things in the story. Again, make sure that you write up the quotations to hammer home the fact that the information comes from a particular sort of historical source.

To deal with the concept of 'points of view' you, of course, need two or more sources to contrast. In a project about evacuation with nine-year-olds we collected accounts from a number of individuals of the arrival of children in Worthing from South London. These accounts included: 'Alice' the young evacuee, a billeting officer, two Worthing children, a Worthing teacher. We also found a diary kept by an extremely crusty old Worthing couple recording their disgust at the idea of children being billeted on them, and the plans made by the town clerk for the reception of evacuees.

We made a full transcription of the accounts. Some older children will be able to do some of this themselves, on the word processor, but it is a time-consuming job and it may be easier to try to find a helpful parent. If all else fails you just might be able to prevail upon the long-suffering and overworked school secretary.

We split the children into groups, one group being evacuees with their teacher, another being billeting officers with the town clerk, while the last group were Worthing families. Each group read and discussed only the account that was relevant to them. The evacuees read 'Alice', the families read 'Old Mr Harris' and young 'Keith', and so on. The children then created their own characters for the role play, drawing on the evidence. We started with the groups acting separately. The evacuees arrived at school on the fateful morning and the teacher got them to the train. The billeting officers were briefed before doing the rounds of the families who had been at home discussing the situation. As we played through the day, the tensions and conflicts of the different interests and emotions of those involved emerged very clearly. Subsequent written work by the children showed an excellent understanding of the situation.

As I have said, for this exercise we used two documentary sources along with the various oral ones because the contrasting of the different sorts of record is an essential part of historical research. We noticed a distinct difference in emphasis between various sorts of wartime record. Accounts written during the war were often, as one might expect, suffused with a certain amount of gloom and desperation, even when they were desperately optimistic. In contrast oral war memories recorded recently were usually positive and even nostalgic. There are obvious reasons for this: the danger and horror of that war is long past and ex-participants can afford to remember the good aspects, like the comradeship and sense of national purpose. Those that still have truly bad memories of the war will usually prefer not to talk about it at all, leaving only the positive accounts for us to hear. Some who had very bad experiences feel the more positive about themselves precisely because they have come through such things, and therefore their accounts sound quite cheerful even when recounting horrors. Lastly we should think about who we are asking. Most living informants were comparatively young during the war, schoolchildren or young adults. To many schoolchildren the war was a great game with real dogfights to watch and bits of crashed plane to collect, and best of all very little school. To young middle-class women the war was a great liberator allowing them to stay out all night, drive lorries and meet lots of uniformed young men. When I have interviewed people who were older at the beginning of the war I have often heard less rosy memories.

Children should be encouraged to discuss *why* accounts differ, and, as I suggested earlier in the chapter, insights gained in this way are directly transferable to written accounts of the oral tradition and contemporary records. Children, and many adults, often tend to believe without question anything in print. It is often easier for them to think about bias and points of view when they have a real person in front of them, as they are much more used to disbelieving people face-to-face.

Further reading

Thompson, P. (1978) *The Voice of the Past: Oral History*. Oxford: OUP.
Humphries, A. (1984) *Handbook of Oral History*. London: Inter-Action.

CHAPTER 7
Documentary Evidence

The regular use of archaeology and oral sources in the writing of history is a comparatively recent phenomenon. Traditionally the skill of the academic historian was research into documents. Work with original written material, however, presents a number of problems with children. Firstly it requires a level of proficiency in reading and comprehension. Vocabulary may be unfamiliar, also styles of handwriting. Secondly, while artefacts often have a practical dimension that trancends time and at least form a starting point for interpretation, documents are often incomprehensible outside their social and cultural context. While objects and people are generally of immediate interest to children, documents often are not. None the less looking at documents is essential, not only because the National Curriculum requires it, but also because they usually get us closer than any other sort of evidence to what actually was going on on a particular day in a particular place.

Much of the document work done in schools at the moment is taken from printed sources. Several major publishers are producing study materials which include extracts from contemporary documents, along with prepared activities. Translations of many suitable works such as Julius Caesar's *The Conquest of Gaul* or the *Anglo-Saxon Chronicle* are readily available in their entirety. There is nothing, however, to beat the 'joy of the chase' experienced when doing real 'detective work' with real original documents. In fact, my experience has been that it is hard to stop once you have started, so addictive is the feeling of finding out about the secret history of your immediate surroundings. Even at Key Stage 1, when the reading skills of the pupils are insufficient for much documentary work, the study of old pictures and photographs is very appropriate and can form a good way of introducing children to written material.

'Real' research is usually only possible on a local basis. In the National Curriculum the Local History Study Unit is an ideal vehicle for it, but local studies can also usefully form a part of other Units, particularly those on Victorian and twentieth-century life.

Local records

Your first move in local research should be to find out what records are available and where they are. The best place to start is usually the local library service. Most county libraries have a local history archive kept in one or more centres, and most have a local history librarian or archivist in charge. The provision is very uneven. While some areas have a purpose-built reading room, full-time staff, microfilm viewers, and easy immediate access to records, other areas have one part-timer, no facilities and little apparent system in their records. It is also difficult to predict exactly what will be kept in your local library, but you should, at least, find most of the following:

Street directories

These have been published for individual towns every three years or so from the latter part of the last century. A directory will list all the streets in the town extant at the time of printing, all the houses in the streets, and the name(s) of the householders. If business was carried out from the address, then the occupation of the householder will be there too.

Old maps

There are usually a reasonable number of large-scale maps of the area going back at least to the mid-nineteenth century, often to much earlier. They usually include tithe maps which give ownership and use of land, early Ordnance Surveys, and sometimes more specialised maps like geological ones or sewer plans.

Local newspapers

Libraries often keep old local newspapers on microfiche or microfilm.

Proceedings of local historical society

These are often worth looking at for interesting areas of study in your neighbourhood and also particulars of where documents can be found.

Census returns

Many local history libraries keep at least some local census returns on microfiche or microfilm. The originals are in the Public Record Office

Census Department (see 'Useful addresses', p. 78). The first census in Britain was held in 1841, and one has been held every ten years since, except in 1941. The 'thirty year rule' applies, so you can look at returns from up to thirty years ago. Returns list all the inhabitants of a house, their ages, sex, family relationship, occupation and place of birth. They are invaluable to social historians.

Old topographical photographs and prints

These are very useful, especially as photographers over the years often seem to choose the same local views, allowing 'then and now' comparisons. Many libraries publish some of their photo collection as postcards.

Local history books

It is surprising how many local histories have been written, sometimes about the most obscure aspects of an area. They range from eccentric antiquarian works written two hundred years ago to neat little booklets published by the library itself. Some of the older ones contain fascinating old traditions based on no evidence; but even these can be very useful when teaching about the need for historical evidence. The local volume of the *Victoria County History* will certainly be available.

Local official records

These are of all sorts. The proceedings of the local Workhouse committees and the Health Board, for instance, often paint graphic pictures.

History files

The library will often keep its own files of newspaper clippings and other material on local issues or the local manifestations of national ones.

Have a friendly talk to the archivist and explain your interest. There will often be exciting and relevant material available which is not on display and which you will hear about only by enthusiastic enquiry. I have yet to meet an archivist who is not an enthusiast and helpful to others who share his or her enthusiasm. The archivist will generally photocopy anything in the records for you, but it may not be possible to do this immediately.

Having practised retrieving and examining documentary material in the local library you are now ready to visit the County Record Office. This will keep many of the same sorts of material as the library, but in greater quantity and for the whole county. If you have already visited the library you will probably already have a list of things you wish to see.

There is a certain etiquette to be observed in a record office. Take pencils and paper for your notes as pens and biros are not usually allowed (in case you accidently mark a valuable document). You will generally have to fill in a request slip for the material you wish to see, which an archivist will then bring to your table. Again, do discuss your work with the archivist. I remember on one occasion spending days trying to find out the history of a particular windmill, yet when I mentioned this in passing to a member of the record office staff he immediately said: 'Of course you have looked at Mr X's work over in Brighton?' At Brighton library I found a neat file containing everything I had painstakingly researched and a lot more.

The local museum will also have documentary material, pictures and history files. Often they are especially keen on 'ephemera', a classification that includes tickets, playbills, posters, leaflets etc.

The most interesting material of all is probably diaries, letters, recipe books and other personal writings. These might be in any of the above locations. Many second-hand bookshops sell old postcards, and these can be interesting both for the pictures and the message on the back.

There are many other sorts of record to be found in many other places, but the best way to find it is to start the trail, and start talking to people. You will find that one thing leads to another.

On the trail of the past

A student of mine, for just a few pence, recently purchased a bundle of old postcards in a charity shop. They proved to be one side of a correspondence between two young women, 'Elsie' and 'Mary', that spanned the war years. He made these a part of a school history project. The class found the old house of 'Elsie', the writer, from the address on the cards (which was fortunately local). They photographed it and, with the help of old maps, identified the changes that had occurred in the street since the war. The history file in the local library contained a map of bombs that had fallen in the borough (many local papers published these in special issues just after VE Day, and sometimes in commemorative issues since then), and this told the children how many of the changes were due to bomb damage and how many to later development. The class also consulted a pre-war census return for the street and found out about Elsie's family. The writer of the letters to Elsie was identified in the postcards only as 'Mary', but in the census return the children found a Mary of about the same age as Elsie who lived three doors away. Was this her friend? If so, why did she move? This led nicely into 'reasons why people move house' (see National Curriculum for geography) and into issues like evacuation, war work and the role of women. The museum had copies of the Public Information leaflets on evacuation, which photocopied nicely, and the children talked to local people who had been evacuated. The school still had its log books from the war years, and the entries for 1940 gave details of the evacuation arrangements.

Of course this study formed only a part of the pupil's work on the war, which in turn was only part of 'Britain since 1930'. Time was limited, and interesting tracks, such as whether Elsie was still alive and available for comment, had to be deferred. The student concerned was able to research just one step ahead of his pupil's questions, only by dint of a heroic commitment of free time and persistence. But he considered his efforts to be worthwhile since it was the tangible link with Elsie that caught his class's imagination. The maps, census returns and log books gave facts: but the cards, with their inconsequential detail interspersed with comments that suddenly revealed the war in the background, gave the children a sense that all the events did not happen in a play, but were once real life to real people.

Organisation

Research through archives is time-consuming and fraught with 'dead-ends'. Though it is often possible, and highly desirable, to arrange a class visit to the local history library or record office, it is clearly impractical for a whole class of primary aged children to do the research. Written material has the great advantage over artefacts that it can be photocopied. This means that the children's work will be largely concerned with interpretation of copied documents in the classroom. Having said this, it is important whenever possible to show original documents, and to make children aware of the processes involved in your research. They must understand that they are actively engaged in a search for history, that there are real questions to be answered, not just artificial ones created for their edification.

Using photographs

As with artefacts, it is necessary to teach method from an early stage. At Key Stage 1, work with photographs is ideal. It is usually not difficult to buy, from the library or local museum, reproduction photographs of local views taken in Victorian or Edwardian times. Go out with a camera and try to take exactly the same view as it is today. Sunday morning early is a good time to go if you do not want to be run over whilst trying to stand in the middle of the road like your Victorian predecessor. You will probably want to enlarge the pictures. The best method to do this is to take a photograph of your postcard and have the result 'blown up'. If you have access to a copying stand this is easy, but I have obtained good results with the card flat on the table, and supporting the camera over it with my elbows on the table. You may have trouble with lighting the card without reflections and I find that the natural light on a window ledge is best. A clear enlargement of a black-and-white photo can also be made with a colour photocopier, and many High Street 'copyshops' have these. Using an ordinary photocopier for reproducing monochrome photos rarely gives good results, and I would advise against using a poor reproduction with young children.

The obvious exercise then is to ask the children to compare the photographs. Tell them to look for similarities as well as differences, and set limits to the task. For example, find five things which have changed and five things that have stayed the same will avoid the queue of children wanting to know if they have finished. Talk through the children's findings as a class, bringing out the detail of changes: 'William has noticed that the shop on the corner is different. Look carefully at the window. What things are for sale in each picture?' Talk about the reasons for changes: Why are there no television aerials in the old picture? Get the children to make 'then and now' drawings on themes like transport, clothing or shops.

It is important to show the children how to find out more by using secondary sources: 'I wondered if all ladies dressed like the one in our photograph in 1910, so I got this book from the library . . .'. You may well find a small piece in a local newspaper of the same period as the photograph that could be read to the children. Again, the children should listen for similarities and differences, and try to understand the concerns of the period. Above all, look for balance in what you bring out. Young children are very apt to decide that it was horrible in the past because there was no television, or wonderful because one did not have to go to school. This is quite natural, but bad history. Cause and consequence and point of view must be continually emphasised. Each piece of evidence must be compared to other pieces, and generalisations should not be made on the basis of one account. I have heard teachers remark that young children need certainties and cannot cope with the historian's continually qualified answers. This has not been my experience. Learning that life is not all 'black and white' is an important lesson that can be taught, and the history class is a very good place to teach it.

Historical learning carries on in parallel to the rest of the curriculum, and it is particularly 'symbiotic' with geography and language work. The photograph work is a good stimulus for descriptive writing when the children have reached the appropriate stage. If possible, take the children to the area where the photos were taken, then they can describe what they can see, smell and hear. The class can imagine that they are standing in the old photograph and describe the scents of horses, the sound of harness and church bells etc.

Using street maps

As you begin to work on street maps in geography, you can do similar exercises in 'then and now' comparison with old maps. With both maps and photographs children can describe a walk through your town in Edwardian times. Look for changes in the social make-up of an area. Many terraced streets that will be listed in the old street directory as the homes of chimney sweeps, bone boilers, tallow melters and 'nightmen' are now thick with BMWs and burglar alarms. Other streets that the census shows as single family homes, with servants and set amongst orchards, are now split into many flats and overlooked by tower blocks.

The name of a street can give you clues about its past. Names like 'Church Walk', or 'Bridgend Road' tend to be traditional ones describing the location. Developers wishing to sell houses try to give the streets names which the prospective class of buyer will find attractive. Thus late Victorian middle-class streets often have names like 'Poole Avenue' or 'Sandown Place', evoking respectable seaside holidays. Mansion flats for well-off single men were in 'Parma Crescent' or 'Byron Court', reflecting the cosmopolitan and artistic tastes of the tenants. Working-class terraces did not need inviting names since the occupants were attracted more by proximity to the factory or low rents. These streets were sometimes named after the builder or often his wife or daughters: 'Jessica Road', 'Amelia Street'. (I have noted that some Gujerati supermarket owners today follow this tradition, and have had children in my class with shops named after them.) Contemporary heroes or battles are often commemorated in street names. Nelson or Wellington are easy to spot, but the battle of Maida, the relief of Ladysmith and the surrender at Sedan are less familiar to us now. As one looks at the proliferation of 'Mandela

Houses' in the 1980s it is worth comparing the phenomenon to the similar 'left-wing hero' cult of Garibaldi in street names from the nineteenth century. (Giuseppe Garibaldi was the victor at Maida, and a great hero of the working classes of London.) 'Local boys made good' have streets named after them, as did the great or not-so-great landowners on whose estates the new developments were made. Sometimes names have changed reflecting a change of social pattern, of use or just of taste over the years.

Using census returns

Census returns are great favourites for computer-based work. Standard school databases can process the returns for an area in a particular year to create statistics such as the average family size, popularity of Christian names, or the number of people born in the area in which they lived. You can try comparing two 'fields', such as occupation and size of family. You can introduce your own sub-classification of social class, based on occupation, and compare it to the number of 'scholars' in the family. Or look at the age of the scholars or youth of the workers. The two main problems with census databases are entering the information and finding an appropriate body of information to compare it to.

There are several ready-made census databases on the market, such as 'Barry 1871' on 'Clipboard'. But it is obviously much better to use local material. However, this means that somebody has the time-consuming job of entering all the information on to the database. Since you are unlikely to be allowed to take your school computer into the local record office, you will have to get photocopies of all the records you wish to use, which will be quite a few if you want a database that is any use. The operation will be even more of a headache if the original enumerator had difficult handwriting (as I know to my cost). The problem can be shared if a number of schools in an area work together to make a database that all of them can use. I know of one or two cases where this has been done, and in each case it proved well worth the considerable effort.

The problem of comparison arises as the 'thirty year rule' means that you cannot use an up-to-date census. The impact of knowing the average family size in Victorian Wandsworth is lost if you cannot say what it is today. The answer to this is fairly obvious: children can carry out their own 'human geography' surveys within the school on the aspects that interest them. I would warn, however, that some parents may not take kindly to too many questions being asked.

Personal or family studies

An alternative to a geographically based study is a personal or family one. If you can obtain a number of documents relating to an individual or family then they can form the basis of research that can then broaden into a study of the period in which they lived. You may well find that your own family can provide birth certificates, ration cards, marriage certificates, photos, letters etc. These can be photocopied and used in class.

Start off by giving a document to a pair of children. They should examine it and answer various questions. When was the document produced? Who does it refer to? What does it tell you about them? Why was it produced? Warn the children to look carefully. Dates shown may be the date of the document, the date of birth of the named person, the date of the Act of Parliament in fulfilment of which the document was produced, or something else. Official documents often contain mistakes which may confuse the issue.

When the individual papers have been examined it is time to try to put them together. The two classic ways of doing this are the family tree and the time line. Find the earliest and latest date mentioned in any of the papers and lay them out in order of production along a table. Add slips of paper to show the dates. Where you have found out another significant date (such as a birth date) by looking at a later document, you should put in a slip of paper to show it. If important national events (such as the last war) occurred within the period, then they should be marked on the timeline.

Photographs may not be dated or named. You can date photos approximately by the technology of the photo itself, and by the costume and surroundings shown on it. Obviously children will need reference books to compare with.

The family tree can be constructed on the board by pooling information. There may be a lot of informed guesswork involved as to relationships and events, especially if you are using personal letters. The text will give clues which children are usually very good at interpreting.

When the children have reconstructed the story of your family as best they can, you can fill in gaps with oral history that you have obtained. Be sure to emphasise the fact if the story you have heard does not quite agree with the documents! Using your own family history has the added advantage that pupils are always very 'nosy' about their teacher. You may get some surprises. I had never noticed until a student pointed it out to me that a letter enclosed with an application for leave, from a member of my family during the war, was a forgery. The student noticed that neither the handwriting nor the use of English matched that of the person supposed to have written it.

Work like the above can lead on to the writing of coherent accounts of the events researched, to role play of the conflicts experienced by the characters and to further research into the wider context of the period. Those interested in Auntie Mary's time at the munitions factory can look at the role of women on the home front, and so on.

Printed materials

As has already been said, there are considerable advantages in using material which has local or personal connections with the children in your class. This should be quite possible with Victorian and later history. Even for the Tudors and Stuarts you may well find a local character about whom the county record office has enough information. Earlier periods are more of a problem and you will probably have to rely exclusively on printed translations of contemporary work. Publications such as John West's *Telltale* series have made available some of the most appropriate material in processed form, and most teachers will avail themselves of this facility. It is, however, always advantageous for the teacher to read as much of the complete work as possible. Penguin publish a number of useful works in good translations, and reading Ceasar, Tacitus, Bede, The Saga of King Harald, Columbus, Pepys etc. will give you a much better feel for the period. Look for local comparisons. You may not find a Saxon document about life in south London but you can compare the immigrations mentioned by Bede with those of this century, thus combining knowledge of Invaders and Settlers with the valuable lesson that England has always been a multi-cultural country. To illustrate the amount of material available I append a list of some books that I have used for Invaders and Settlers.

Sources of primary documents for teaching 'Ivaders and Settlers'

The Romans
Ceasar (Trans 1951) *The Conquest of Gaul* (Trans Handford). Harmondsworth: Penguin.
Pp.97–115 deal with Ceasar's two invasions of Britain. The book is in the General's own words, though he refers to himself in the third person.
Tacitus (1948) *The Agricola and the Germania* (Trans Mattingly). Harmondsworth: Penguin.
Pp.60–7 are about 'the geographical position and inhabitants of

Britain'. Pp.68-92 are about the campaigns of the Governor and General, Agricola in Britain. The book is by Agricola's son-in-law Tacitus.

The Saxons
Gildas (1978) *The Ruin of Britain* (Ed. John Morris). Chichester: Phillimore.
This is almost the only existing document contemporary to the Saxon invasions. Gildas is very difficult to understand but he does give an account of how the Saxons got here. J.N.L. Myres The English Settlements *compares Gildas with other evidence in an interesting way.*
Nennius (1980) *British History and the Welsh Annals* (Ed. John Morris). Chichester: Phillimore.
A selection of earlier writings collected by a Welsh monk in the eighth century. Pp.28-33 are about early dealings with the saxons, p.35 deals with the campaigns of King Arthur, and gives the Welsh Annal entries that mention Arthur.
Bede (1955) *A History of the English Church and People* (Trans Sherley-Price). Harmondsworth: Penguin.
The first real history of the English. Much of it is relevant, but in particular, pp.51-8 are about the coming of the Angles, Saxons and Jutes to Britain.
Savage, A. (1982) *The Anglo-Saxon Chronicles.* London: Papermac.
Early English timeline entries begin at 485 AD and go on to 1153. The early ones are retrospective but the later ones are contemporary. Particularly exciting is the entry for 793 which records the first great Viking raid on Britain.
Alexander, M. (1966) *The Earliest English Poems.* Harmondsworth: Penguin.
'The Battle of Maldon' is about a fight with the Vikings.
'Riddles' are popular with children.
'The Wife's Complaint' gives a woman's point of view (difficult).

The Vikings
Savage, A. (1982) *The Anglo-Saxon Chronicles.* London: Papermac.
(See entry above.) Many entries after 800 AD give an English view of the Vikings.
Alexander, M. (1966) *The Earliest English Poems.* London: Penguin.
(See entry above – 'The Battle of Maldon'.)

Sturlasson, S. (1971) *King Harald's Saga*. Harmondsworth: Penguin.
The life of Harald Hadraada gives an exciting insight into the world of one of the last great Vikings. Harald died trying to gain the English crown at Stamford Bridge in 1066.

Useful addresses

Public Record Office, Chancery Lane, London WC2 1LR.
Public Record Office, Census Section, Portugal Street, London WC2.
Public Record Office, Ruskin Avenue, Kew, Richmond, Surrey TW9 4DU.
Greater London Record Office, 40 Northampton Road, London EC1R 0HB.
Old Greater London Schools records kept here. There is also a photograph section.
Federation of Family History Societies, c/o Benson Room, Birmingham and Midland Institute, Margaret Street, Birmingham B3 3BS.
These people publish a list of where all copies of census returns are held within the UK.

CHAPTER 8
Planning a History Study Unit

To have lots of bright ideas for making history challenging and interesting is all very well, but nowadays it is not enough. There is a solid body of content that must, by law, be covered. Facts matter. What daunts many teachers is the sheer amount that must be covered. Over the primary years, ten Units must be taught, spanning around 6,000 years of history. 'Invaders and Settlers' alone covers a period from 55 BC to 1066 AD. Pupils must be taught about political, economic, social, religious and cultural aspects of the period (the so-called PESC formula, see Programme of Study for Key Stage 2). They must learn about the lives of men and women, and about their social, cultural, religious and ethnic diversity.

Along with the chronology and knowledge of key events the children are required to develop their concepts and skills. Ideas of sequence, cause and effect, time and change, points of view, evidence and interpretation must all be used in increasingly complex ways. Along with research skills, the ability to express and communicate historical information must not be neglected. Use of information technology must also be incorporated. In all these aspects of learning pupils are expected to progress through levels of attainment, and the teacher is expected to assess the progress of each individual. Meanwhile, of course, the National Curriculum has provided the busy teacher and her class with one or two other things to do, in the shape of mathematics, science, language, design and technology, geography, art, RE, PE etc.

To achieve all these things a considerable amount of planning will be necessary. Much of this planning may be at whole-school level to ensure that the pupil covers the full range of content and emphasis through the primary years. In many places planning at district or local authority level is taking place so that resources can be pooled and opportunities provided. Many schools have gratefully received the published schemes such as Longman's *Sense of History* packs, and some are using them to the exclusion of anything else.

There is a danger that the teacher, deluged with demands, will rely more and more on others to provide packaged lessons and activities. This, I feel, is a bad thing, *if carried too far*, because:

(a) History is about forming identity through the relation of past and present. The diversity of our children demands a diversity of approaches. Children who live in different areas and have different backgrounds and abilities will require different emphases and examples if they are to place themselves within the pattern of our culture.
(b) The shining glory of our primary education has always been the personal involvement and enthusiasm of the class teacher. You, as the teacher, are more likely to communicate excitement if you are teaching lessons that you have created yourself; about things you have enjoyed discovering.

The published schemes often provide a good start for planning. The writers have done much research and selected appropriate content. Printed documentary sources are often handled quite well. Increasingly, good IT materials are being produced, notably by BBC/ Longman Logotron and in National Council for Educational Technology projects. But work with artefacts, oral history, visits and local history are still best planned at the local or class level.

To plan a Study Unit effectively the teacher must prepare herself well in advance and take into consideration a number of factors before deciding what to do. We shall now examine these factors.

Know your area

The school is, or should be, an organic part of the local community. The locality, and what goes on in it, is your greatest resource. As a teacher you need to know about the history of your area. To acquire such knowledge there are a number of steps that you can take:

1. Go to the local library and read any materials on the area. Often the library itself will have produced booklets and reference files. Make notes on the possible local connections to the relevant Study Units, and any possible foci for local history studies. Find out the addresses of the local history society, archaeological group and any other relevant local organisation.
2. Go to the local museum and find out what they have, both on display and in store. Again, look for links with the National Curriculum. Find out the name of the education officer or interested curator, and talk to them about the services they

provide and the ideas that they have to offer. Ask if any oral history collecting has taken place and if they know of good informants about local matters.
3. Make sure that your school is on the mailing list for exhibitions. If, as sometimes happens, the school receives such information but immediately buries it under a pile of paper on the staff room table, arrange for it to be sent personally to you, and check it regularly.
4. Look at Ordnance Survey maps. Examine modern ones for ancient monuments, sites of battles or intriguing place names. Inspect old ones in the library and archives to find the changes that the area has gone through.
5. Walk the streets around the school. Look up, above the shop fronts, at the local architecture. Look out for old street furniture, Victorian post boxes, converted gaslights or horse troughs. Walk along any waterways, noticing the marks of tow ropes on canal bridges or signs set up by the canal company.
6. Read the local newspaper and start your own file of interesting cuttings.
7. Above all *talk to people*. Pensioners walking their dogs, roadsweepers, landlords of pubs, and factory managers have all given me valuable material with very little prompting, once they knew that I was a fellow enthusiast.

Note that all the above should be carried out as a matter of course by a good teacher, so that when the time comes to plan history work the information, or at least where to find it, will be at your fingertips.

Know your pupils

I include this subtitle only for the sake of completeness since it is second nature to the professional primary school teacher. I mean only that the particular interests and enthusiasms, the background and family of the children in your care are relevant to the approach that you make to a study. Move from what the pupils know to what they do not know. Use their interests as a link to broaden their horizons. The only caveat that I would include here is to beware of focusing on the experience of a particular child *without the child's permission*. Few children would object to their parent's collection of railway memorobilia, for instance, making them the centre of attention; but some may feel uncomfortable at any 'difference' between them and the rest of the class being brought out. It is a matter of common courtesy to seek their opinion.

Know the statutory and local requirements

The National Curriculum for history is quite a simple and straightforward document. The statutory requirements mean no more, and no less, than what they say, and leave a great deal of leeway for individual interpretation. You *must* cover all that is layed down in a unit, but often the emphases are left to you. You must be balanced in your approach, checking the Key Elements on p.15 of the document; but the balance is achieved across the Key Stage (see p.16 of the document). You must familiarise children with all the different sources of information, but the emphasis will vary with the period being studied: for instance oral history would contribute much to 'Britain since 1930' or to a Key Stage 1 project, whereas archaeology would be an appropriate source of material for 'Invaders and Settlers'.

A 'whole-school approach' is now necessary, to a greater or lesser extent, and you will have to work with your colleagues to achieve balance through the school. Hilary Cooper (1992) in *The Teaching of History* (published by David Fulton) has excellent chapters on the subject of planning. In many areas there are also local authority guidelines.

Know the period

For many teachers, a knowledge of the period being studied is the most difficult problem, particularly for those who have not studied history at a higher level. Even those with degrees in history are often rather 'at sea' outside 'their period'. None of us is an expert on every area of history and teaching methods that require an investigative approach demand a wider knowledge from the teacher than the old 'text book' methods. The first instinct of many with whom I have worked is to collect all the children's books on the relevant period in the school and read them. You will, of course, need to do this at some point, but I feel that it is difficult to evaluate these books without first gaining an adult and a rather more academic view. There is no short cut to this: you do have to do some reading; but clearly you will not have the time to read through a lengthy booklist at the same time as preparing work in all the other subjects. Most schools will have a co-ordinator for history, who can do some of the planning for you. But nobody can hand you the knowledge and understanding that you will need on a plate. I would suggest the following programme as an example of the minimum preparation necessary the first time that you teach a Unit:

1. Buy a 'big' history book like Morgan's *The Oxford History of England*, obtainable in paperback. Books like this have chapters on the periods written by scholars who are acknowledged experts in the field. Read the relevant chapter and start to make your own timeline of the period. Check that you have on it everything mentioned in the National Curriculum document, and anything you find relevant, interesting, local or exciting. Get the dates sorted out, and the prominent figures and events. Check over your local notes and look for connections, noting anniversaries that will come up during the term. This exercise should give you a general picture and a list of possible foci to follow up. Use the bibliography to the chapter to locate books on specific areas and note also the title of the writer's own main works on the period.
2. Let us suppose that you are interested in the Romans. You have read Peter Salway's chapter in the above mentioned volume and obtained from the library his major work *The Romans in Britain* (Oxford University Press). You may observe that it is a long book and that there is no time to read it all at this stage: so be selective. Use the index and the bibliography. Look right through the index for local placenames and names of figures that you have already noted as characters in the story you wish to tell, and look up the events that you have chosen to concentrate on. Photocopy or make notes. Use the bibliography to tell you where to find out more about the areas that particularly interest you, and the primary documentary sources that the author has used. From Salway, for instance, you could learn that Tacitus' *Germania* is available in translation in the Penguin Classics series, as is Julius Caesar's *The Invasion of Gaul* (which also tells the story of the invasion of Britain). You can be reasonably certain that historians of Salway's stature will have used most of the relevant sources. Check these books in the library to see how you might use them with children of the age and ability that you are teaching.
3. A painless way of 'getting into the period' and finding background material, is to find good historical novels to use as your own bedtime reading. These might be children's books that are possibles to use in class. Some children's fiction such as Rosemary Sutcliff's *Eagle of the Ninth* or *The Lantern Bearers* (both Puffin paperbacks) make very acceptable adult reading, and are full of accurate period detail. You might try something like Colleen McCulloch's *The First Man in Rome* if you prefer more

meat. Your local library will have stacks of such books, and you can learn a lot by reading them.

Assess your pupils

There can be no meaningful planning without previous assessment of the childrens' historical understanding. As the National Curriculum becomes fully operational, assessment, in its simplest form, based on the Statements of Attainment, will be carried out as a matter of course as a continuing process. You should receive a profile of the individuals' achievements from their previous teacher who will also keep examples of the childrens' work. You will be expected to continue this record. All teachers know, however, even if our political masters do not, that what a child can do today, and what they will remember tomorrow, are not always the same thing. This is particularly true when a summer holiday has intervened. You may well, therefore, wish to carry out your own tests to find out, for instance, how many children in your class can 'suggest reasons why people in the past acted as they did' (NC History AT1 L2). Often the best way to carry out simple planning assessments is to read a story and ask questions afterwards. This may be done orally, or you may require a pictorial or written answer from the children. This sort of assessment is 'rough and ready' and should not be taken as a final judgement on the individual's ability. But it can show you the average level of the class, and it can identify groups within the class at different levels. Write a list of types of activity that will consolidate the skills and concepts that the pupils have already acquired so that you can extend these to the next level.

Look for links with the rest of the curriculum

The fact that the emphasis within the National Curriculum is on discrete subjects does not preclude 'killing two birds with one stone' by making links with other curriculum areas where this is educationally justified. It will often be possible, for instance, to fulfil your objectives for language at the same time as those for history, since most of the results of your historical enquiry must be communicated through the medium of language. It is nigh on impossible to carry out a local study in history without carrying out a geographical one in parallel. One cannot compare the past and present of the locality without enquiring into its current characteristics. As we have seen, work with artefacts involves technological understanding, and whenever possible this should be planned to coincide with the requirements of the design and technology curriculum. If you plan for these links from the start, then you can save valuable classroom time, as well as providing the child with a much more holistic view of the world.

Research secondary sources, ava and IT

Do not forget that secondary sources in the form of history books and work packs, children's fiction, television and radio programmes, computer simulations and databases are all an important part of history teaching though their examination is beyond the scope of this book. Library services often make up project libraries: use them if available. The National Council for Educational Technology (NCET) publish information about the use of IT. Check current timetables for TV broadcasts. Never use any material that you have not seen and evaluated first.

Planning the sessions

The Primary School Curriculum is now very full and you will have a limited amount of time to devote to history work. You will know the number and length of the sessions you have for the Unit. If you have found good cross-curricular links then this may have extended the time available. I like to plan with the aid of the timeline of the period that I have prepared.

Take a large sheet of paper and rule a line horizontally across the middle. Enter the beginning and end dates of the period that you are studying at each end of the line. Mark suitable graduations along the line for the intervening years. Write on the key events mentioned in the National Curriculum document and any other episodes, local or national that you have decided to teach about.

Take your list of priorities in skills and concepts and marry them to the material that you have researched. For instance, when studying 'Invaders and Settlers' you might need to teach the children to 'give a reason for an historical event or development' (AT1 L3b), and also to 'make deductions from historical sources' (AT3 L3). Through Salway you have discovered Julius Caesar's account of his invasion of Britain, and also accounts by Strabo and Tacitus of the wealth of the country. You would also note that teaching about the reasons for the Roman Invasion is a statutory requirement. You could, therefore, achieve these three separate goals by planning an activity suitable to your class which involves looking at the documentary accounts mentioned and, through discussion, role play and research, forming hypotheses about whether Caesar really came just to punish the British for helping his enemies or whether he had other motives.

As you plan activities like this, write them in bubbles or boxes on the sheet and connect them to your timeline. When you have dealt with your priority concepts and skills, turn to any other elements emphasised in the instructions for teaching the Unit which you have not yet covered. Again try to connect the required teaching points to good resources that you have found, and ensure that you plan activities that reinforce and extend the child's historical understanding as layed down in the Attainment Targets. For instance, in 'Invaders and Settlers' you need to talk about 'everyday life in town and country' and 'houses and home life'. A teacher in West Cornwall would immediately think of using the remains of a Romano-British village at Chysauster; in West Sussex we have the Roman Palace at Fishbourne and the villa at Bignor; a London teacher has the Ordnance Survey map of Roman London, and so on.

Do not forget to leave time for connecting lessons, when you will use narrative, good old-fashioned story-telling, to cover the gaps left by the activities. A timeline on the wall is, I think, essential in every primary school history Unit, to visually reinforce and consolidate the child's ideas of chronology and sequence.

Make sure that you have, as far as possible, achieved balance between political, economic, technological, scientific, social, religious and cultural elements of the period. Make sure that you have material about the experiences of men *and* women *and* children.

Once you have created a list of lessons, think of the most effective order in which to teach them. A strictly chronological approach may not always be the best one, and you have your timeline to keep things in order. You will want to start with something that catches the children's interest, and which makes them want to follow through and learn more. As I have already suggested, one interesting artefact, or one old postcard, if properly handled can lead to an enquiry from which the whole Unit can emerge.

Individual lessons should be planned to:

1. Achieve continuity and progression through the skills and concepts in the Attainment Targets. Where individuals or groups within the class have special needs because of their greater or lesser ability in some areas, your planned activities must include variations to ensure that they are able to progress as well.
2. Deliver some solid and accurate historical information.
3. Use the most varied, interesting and appropriate resources available.

4. Have assessment built into the activities. You must know at the beginning of the lesson what you expect each child to achieve, and at the end you must know to what extent your expectations have been realised. You may be assessing a 'product' in the form, perhaps, of written work, or you may assess the child visually or orally as they work. If you do the latter then you must have worked out the simple indicators that you are looking for, and you must have prepared a record sheet to keep track of your observations.
5. Lessons should also be fun.

A final word

I end this book with a heartfelt plea to overworked and harassed teachers and students who, I hope, may read it. For the non-specialist, good history teaching will be hard work. It will require a personal commitment of time and energy, some personal research and the personal acquisition of some new skills. I beg you to make that commitment, as the rewards for you and your pupils will be immense. A taste for history is a joy for life. It makes the world around you more accessible and comprehensible. It puts your own life in perspective. As you explore your locality it will magically turn into an open book full of cryptic little messages from the people who lived there before you. As I walk back across the park from the supermarket I can see a discolouration in the grass that marks the course of a brook, crossing which William Cowerson, the last smuggler shot in Sussex, met his fate in 1832. As I sit down in my armchair in the front room, the newly stripped floorboards show hollows made by hobnail boots at just the place where my feet rest. I like to think that they were made by the boots of George Shimmell, a joiner, who lived in this house from 1870 till the early twentieth century, as he sat down after a hard day. Learning to weigh the evidence before you accept Caesar's word on why he came to Britain may help you to look critically at the points of view of modern politicians. Above all, I maintain that learning history can liberate us from the imposition of other people's ideas about who we are and where we came from. Do not take the word of the tabloid press or their opponents in the political spectrum about what it means to be British, or to be a woman or a man or to be black or white. There is enough history for all of us, and learning to deal with it in a critical, enquiring, logical manner can only make us, and our pupils, more tolerant and responsible citizens, able to judge the merits of different opinions, to see the value of our own way of life and of other ones, and to take a proper and considered part in the democratic life of our country.

Further reading

National Curriculum Council (1991) *History in the National Curriculum* (statutory orders and non-statutory guidelines). London: Department of Education and Science.

Cooper, H. (1992) *The Teaching of History*. London: David Fulton Publishers.

Index

Acquiring artefacts, 21-22
Aerial photographs, 24
Alcock, L., 16
Analysing Artefacts, 11-13
Ancient Greece, 37, 58
Archaeology, 23-29, 45
   contexts, 24
   levels, 25
   visiting digs, 28
Assessment, 84
Black History, 5
Blyth, J., 9
Britain since 1930, 58, 71
Building, 54
Butser Hill, 45
Carbon dating, 26
'Cavemen', 48
Census returns, 68, 74
Cissbury Hill, 29
Concepts, 64, 79
Condition of objects, 17-18
Cooking, 54
County Record Office, 70
Cross-curricular links, 84
Clay, 14-15
Dendrochronology, 27
Documentary sources (printed), 76-78
Dying, 53
Ephemera, 70
Evidence, 3
Family studies, 75-76
Field walking, 22
Fines, J., 9
Flint working, 48-51
Food, 54

Grid lines, 24
Grimes graves, 51
Harvey, D, 52
H.M.I. report 1989, 8
Hodges, H., 16
Historical fiction 83
'History Debate', 2-7
History teaching in the past, 4-5
Human Origins, 10
'Ice Man', 17
Inscriptions, 19-20
   country of origin, 19
   handwritten inscriptions, 19
   manufacturer's names, 19
   patent numbers, 19
Institute of Archaeology, 51
Invaders and Settlers, 58
Iron Age, 45
IT, 85
'Landmarks in history', 6
Lesson planning, 85-87
'Lindow Man', 17
Loan collections, 43
Local records
   census returns, 68, 74
   history files, 69
   local history library, 68
   local history society, 68
   local newspapers, 68
   photos and prints, 69
   old maps, 68
   street directories, 68
Local History study unit, 67
Margaret Thatcher, 6
Metals, 15-16

casting, 16
corrosion, 15
forging, 15
hammering, 15
rolling, 16
Museums, 33–44
commercial, 37
cost, 35, 36, 37
local, 35
national, 36
oral work in, 40–41
planning a visit, 39
reasons for going, 34
specialist, 38
when to visit, 34
where to go, 35–38
National Curriculum, 3, 7, 9, 10, 23, 37, 64, 67, 79, 82
Observational drawing, 40
Oral History
finding informants, 58–59
interview technique, 62–63
using informants, 60–62
using material, 63–66
Oral tradition, 57–58
Organic materials, 17, 26
Pollen analysis, 27
Points of View, 3, 64–65
Pottery, 14–15, 17
experiments, 51–53
samian ware, 52
votive offerings, 52

Phosphate analysis, 27
Photographs, 71–73
Replicas, 23
Research
area, 80
period, 82
Reynolds, P., 46
Role play, 23–24
Secondary sources, 31
Sequencing, 64
Social function of objects, 20
Spinning, 53
Spoil heaps, 22, 24
Stone Age, 46
Storytelling, 8
Street maps, 73
Street names, 73
Sturt, G., 16
Style of objects, 18
Technology of objects, 14–17
Thompson, F., 31
Topics, 8
Trenches, 24
Tudors and Stuarts, 58
Victorian Washdays, 30–31
'Victorian values', 2–3
Weaving, 53
West, J., 9
Women's History, 5
Wood, 16–17
Worksheets, 39, 42

For Product Safety Concerns and Information please contact our EU
representative GPSR@taylorandfrancis.com
Taylor & Francis Verlag GmbH, Kaufingerstraße 24, 80331 München, Germany

www.ingramcontent.com/pod-product-compliance
Lightning Source LLC
Chambersburg PA
CBHW070736230426
43669CB00031B/2534